EXODUS

THE ROAD TO FREEDOM

IN A DECONSTRUCTED WORLD

DAVID CAMPBELL

TABLE OF CONTENTS

Author's Preface   1

Foreword   5

Introduction   9

1	Fate or freedom: two choices for today's world	15
2	The covenant of freedom	35
3	Freedom from the power of sin	45
4	Freedom from the law's condemnation	55
5	Freedom and new life in the Spirit	71
6	Freedom and the fulfilling of the law	97
7	Freedom and the state	109
8	Freedom, the weak and the strong	117
9	Freedom, race and slavery	133
10	Freedom, sex and marriage	147
11	Freedom, wives and husbands	167
12	Freedom, parents and children	181
13	Freedom in the church	187
14	Lessons in freedom from the pandemic	201

About the Author   211

Other Titles   213

AUTHOR'S PREFACE

In 1983, I submitted a PhD thesis to the University of Durham titled "Christian Freedom according to Paul." For decades, it sat on my bookshelf gathering dust. The heart of it informed much of my theology and preaching, but I did nothing with the text itself. Until the day came when I realized that freedom has become a defining issue in our culture, even as very few people understand what true freedom really is.

It's not easy to turn an academic thesis into a book readable by the average person, but this is my attempt. I'm driven by the fact that postmodernism threatens to pull western civilization back into a terrible world it left behind two thousand years ago, the world of fate. Christ did not come to bring political liberty or military deliverance. On the cross, he won instead what might be called an ironic victory. He triumphed through his sacrifice. But as a result, he now reigns over the entire universe, seated at the Father's right hand. His sacrifice has made the way to freedom possible. But in order to find that road and walk in it, we have to understand what freedom is, and that is what I try to explain in this book.

I am grateful for Pastor Matt Chandler's willingness to read the manuscript and write a very gracious foreword. I want to acknowledge the proofreading assistance and helpful suggestions of Pastor Evan Sustar of Anderson, South Carolina. And I would like to express my deep gratitude to our friends Alastair and Debbie Taylor of Rothbury, England for a gift which made possible the production of this book by the ever-capable hands of the creative team at davidandbrook.com of Zeeland, Michigan.

Finally, I wish to honor my wife Elaine, who pushed and prodded me to write this book until all my resistance was gone. I am grateful for her willingness to give up her freedom to marry me, leave home and country behind, and devote herself to the raising of eight children, all the while selflessly giving herself to the call of God on our lives.

I hope this book helps you understand freedom in a deeper way, and in so doing draws you into the way of the cross, the new exodus, the road out of Egypt and into the Promised Land.

Soli Deo gloria. To God alone be the glory.

FOREWORD

MATT CHANDLER

That the Kingdom of God is "in our midst" means at least that we must wrestle with the counterintuitive nature of belonging to the Kingdom. After all, the King of the Kingdom flipped everything on its head on that Mount of Beatitudes in Northern Israel two thousand years ago. It was there we learned that it's not the rich that the Kingdom will belong to but the poor in spirit, not the comfortable that will be comforted but those who mourn. The merciful and meek, the hungry and pure in heart, the peacemakers and the persecuted, the Kingdom is not only theirs but they are "blessed." Looking back across the last two millennia we see this is exactly how the Kingdom has gone from the smallest of all seeds to a tree where the birds lodge. From Jerusalem to every continent on earth the Kingdom has expanded through the joyful sacrifice and suffering of God's people, their steadfastness in persecution and pain and their belief that Jesus' Kingdom is ultimate reality.

This counterintuitive Kingdom sets us at odds with the prevailing cultures of our day and requires us to embrace our oddity. Our faith is at its healthiest and best when it's counter-cultural. We are meant to get our definitions and understanding of reality from God's written word and not from the values and language of our day. Where we acquiesce to the cultural drift we miss out on the power and presence of God. This is significant because of the near constant comments and appeals from Christians about "rights" or "freedoms" that have not been formed by the scriptures but the current cultural moment. Freedom has become synonymous with expressive individualism and many a Christian has fallen prey to the bondage this belief causes.

I first encountered David Campbell in his work with G. K. Beale on the book of Revelation. His intellect and scholarship stand out immediately but he also writes as a man who has been in the trenches of ministry, who knows what it is like to mourn with God's people and long for their maturity, power and depth. David takes us into a robust conversation on what true freedom is, helps us see our "rights" for what they are and applies it beautifully to church, marriage, race, politics, the pandemic and more. This book gets us back to the reality of the Kingdom and lets us live in the oddity that breaks bondage and overthrows the work of the devil.

INTRODUCTION

The Bible as a whole is God's charter of freedom. It contains two separate but interrelated stories of liberation, the exodus through the Red Sea from the slavery of Egypt into the Promised Land, and the exodus through the cross from the bondage of sin and death into the kingdom of God. It is easy to see the original exodus as a story of freedom, but it is just as important to realize the New Testament contains its own exodus, one which is the actual fulfillment of the original.

The Old Testament exodus was freedom from slavery in Egypt, but at the same time freedom for service to Yahweh in the Promised Land. The New Testament exodus has a similar pattern. It is freedom from the kingdom of darkness and the the slavery of sin and death into the kingdom of God, where we have freedom for obedience to God and his law. As Paul puts it: "He has delivered us from the domain of darkness and transferred us to the kingdom of his beloved Son, in whom we have redemption, the forgiveness of sins" (Col. 1:13-14).

The similarity between the exodus of the Old and New Testaments begins in Acts with the portrayal of Christ as the prophet like Moses who is to come. According to Ac. 3:22; 7:37, Jesus is the fulfillment of Moses' declaration in Deut. 18:15 that God would raise up a prophet like him. The idea comes to its height in Revelation, which tells the story of salvation in Christ in the form of a new exodus, in which God's children are delivered from Babylon, transported into a wilderness where they are protected for 42 months (a number associated with the years the Israelites spent in Sinai) and eventually delivered into the Promised Land of the New Jerusalem.

Any understanding of Christian freedom has to be structured around two fundamental truths. It is freedom from something and freedom for something. You can't understand one without understanding the other.

On the first point, Christian freedom is freedom from the power of sin and death, as well as freedom from the just condemnation of the law. On the second point, Christian freedom is freedom by the power of the Spirit for obedience to God's law, as that law should truly be understood. The law, when properly comprehended, points the way to a variety of practical applications. It shows us how to find Christian freedom in a number of different situations in life. As citizens, it shows us the meaning of freedom in relation both to fellow citizens and to the powers of the state. As members of the local church, it shows us the meaning of freedom in relation to true spiritual authority, and also freedom in relation to one another as diverse members of the body. As employees, it shows us the meaning of freedom in relation to employers. As those who are, are not or are not yet married, it shows us the meaning of freedom in relation to the marriage relationship. As wives and husbands, it shows us the meaning of freedom in relation to the marriage covenant between a man and a woman. As parents and children, it shows us the meaning of freedom in relation to the family.

We live in a world which understands freedom primarily as the ability to do what we want to do, with the minimum of interference from anyone else. But as we will show, that is a dead end street in which everyone competes for the biggest share of the pie, and few feel really content or truly free. Postmodernism, in its current expression as social justice or critical theory, is a classic example of a system which promises freedom but cannot deliver it. The reason for this is clear. It is the contemporary manifestation of a way of thinking which dominated the ancient world, was challenged and dethroned by Christianity and is now staging a spectacular comeback. Once the world falls into this trap, freedom is lost and fate rules supreme.

But God offers a way out of it — an exodus as real in its ability to bring freedom as the road on which Moses trod through the Red Sea, across the wilderness and into the Promised Land. This freedom is different from anything the world has conceived. It's a strange freedom which begins by calling us to give up everything we have. Yet in return, God promises us a liberty far broader, deeper and long-lasting than anything this world can give us. It is a freedom to lay down our lives in love for God and others. It is a freedom which, in the words of Jim Elliot, who lost his life for the gospel, causes us to lose what we cannot keep to gain what we cannot lose.

The kingdom of God is a place where the values of this world are turned upside down, and in few respects is this more clearly true than in its understanding of freedom. In a world desperately seeking freedom but finding little more than new forms of slavery, the kingdom we preach has the answers the world needs.

But to preach it accurately and faithfully, and to have God back us up, we need to find out what Christian freedom really is, for the sad truth is that even Christians often don't understand it or take true possession of it. And what you don't have, you can't tell others about.

So with that in mind, let's start on our journey. The exodus is about to begin.

ONE

FATE OR FREEDOM: TWO CHOICES FOR TODAY'S WORLD

The questions humanity has struggled with through the ages are much the same. How did the world come to be? How can we know this world? Can we know beyond what we can see physically around us? Who or what is God? Can we know God? Can we even know ourselves? Who are we? What is our relationship to the world in which we live? Are we determined by forces beyond our control, or are we free? If we are free, what is the basis for our freedom in an apparently random universe?

Human wisdom, broadly speaking, has given two answers to these questions, summarized in their greatest representatives, Plato and Aristotle. One is that the cosmos boils down to one great spiritual or metaphysical reality often called Mind. This cosmic Mind is impersonal, runs through all reality and determines the course of our being. In fact, we are all part of it in some way or another. Sometimes this is linked to a belief in reincarnation or some form of immortality of the soul, sometimes to belief in an undefined spiritual world beyond the material world that we cannot truly understand. The second alternative is the opposite: the cosmos boils down to material reality alone. Everything in it, including us, is nothing more than a random collection of atoms. Nothing survives death. There is no truly spiritual dimension to life. Human consciousness itself is reduced to the result of a series of chemical reactions.

Both approaches, however, do agree on several things. First, that the cosmos is eternal. There is no explanation for how it came to be. It just is, and always will be. Second, in spite of the odd failed attempt to prove the contrary, there is ultimately no such thing as freedom. Whether we are ultimately determined by the actions of an impersonal Mind or by the random movements of atoms, there is no rational explanation for genuine human freedom. We live in a fated world in which there is no such thing as free choice or the power to determine our future.

Both approaches are rooted and grounded in the thought of ancient Greece. Civilizations long predating Greece laid the foundations, but Greece provided the clarity. Everything since then, at least in the western world, and outside of Christianity, is some kind of explanation or variation of the alternatives proposed by Greek religion and philosophy in the millennium before Christ. Our contention is that postmodernism, as expressed in social justice or critical theory, far from being something new, is nothing more than a product of this ancient fatalistic way of thinking.

All human thinking outside of Biblical revelation is rooted and grounded in fatalism. Where then is the way to freedom? Let's go back to the starting point and re-examine this central issue of freedom, and let's do so in the hope of applying what we've found to the social, cultural, political and philosophical environment we find ourselves in today. In doing so, we'll find two things. First, there is nothing really modern about postmodernism and its current manifestation, social justice or critical theory. And second, postmodernism provides no path to freedom.

TWO WAYS OF UNDERSTANDING TIME

Under this and the next two headings, I summarize themes discussed at length by Margaret Visser in her book titled *Beyond Fate*. I encourage you to read the book yourself if you want a much fuller understanding of how these ideas developed in the ancient world of Greece and Rome.

One of the many common phrases we use today is that of the time line. At church, at home or at our place of business we are encouraged to develop a time line and move along it to a point of completion. But how often do we stop to ponder why we view time as a line? The fact is we view time as a line along which events move like vehicles on a road. If we drew a diagram, we might draw past time as a solid line, the present as a dot on the line, and future time as a series of dots, representing the uncertainty of future events. This is a helpful way of picturing time and events. But it is important to remember that time does not exist outside of people. The events occurring along the line involve the lives of people, past and present, the decisions they take, and the consequences of them. The direction of the line is affected by the decisions taken by people according to their free will and power to do what they want, whether for good or for evil. This is the way the Bible understands time. But there is another way, birthed in ancient Greece but also known to the other ancient near eastern civilizations, a way understood today in Hinduism, Buddhism, new age religion, postmodernism and critical theory. This illuminates the fact that, contrary to what people say, there are not many religions to choose from today; there are really only two alternatives. As

C.S. Lewis pointed out many years ago, these are embodied in Judaeo-Christianity and Hinduism, all others being imitations or heresies of one or the other. Whether in ancient Greece, modern Hinduism or postmodern philosophy, the alternative view to Christianity takes the following form. What if we understood this line of time as existing independently of people? It is something there, something given before anything else existed, before even God or the gods existed. We do not know where it came from, but it represents the foundation of existence and cannot be tampered with or changed, by humanity or even by the gods. It takes on a life of its own. People fit into the pattern of events as they move along the line. They are caught up in something beyond their control. Hinduism calls this karma, and the Greeks called it fate.

THE BLUEPRINT OF FATE

For the Greeks and other ancient civilizations (the Indians, Sumerians, Babylonians and Assyrians), fate was a blueprint, a gigantic design laid out in advance. No one could escape from its grasp. It was impersonal and, therefore, without any court of appeal or without any mercy. Even the gods, with their supernatural powers, could not defy fate. Fate was conceived of in two ways, a line and a circle. A person's life was represented by a line or thread. The events of our lives move along a predetermined path and eventually the line or thread is cut, representing the moment of death. This thinking still occurs today, every time someone reads the fate of a person from the lines on their hand, including the line of life and where it ends. According to the Greeks, the time lines of life were controlled by the three Furies, supernatural beings who policed the lines, visiting a terrible retribution on anyone, human or god, trying to stray from the path fate decreed for them. A second way the Greeks pictured fate was by joining the two ends of the line together. Fate now represents a circle or boundary beyond which we cannot move. The circle could represent the fate of an individual. The boundaries of the circle are the limits assigned to that person by fate. The circle easily becomes a prison. Tolkien's ring is a tremendous symbol of fate. It is a circle which binds or dooms those inside it. Freedom can only be achieved by destruction of the ring. The Greek version of the story would have ended differently, for no one could have challenged the power of fate. The ring would certainly have triumphed. Only someone influenced by the Bible like Tolkien could have written a story where freedom existed to destroy the power of fate. That we will talk about shortly. The circle can also represent the world in its totality, the sum total of all of our fates. This circle is then divided up into portions, representing the "lot" or fate of each person.

FATE AND HONOR

The Greek word for fate is *moira*, meaning a portion, something divided out from the whole. It can also refer to a portion of meat cut from the roast. Fate can thus be represented by a pie, cut into pieces. Three things are significant. First, the pie represents all there is. There isn't any more to be had. Second, you can only have the piece you have been offered, just like you can only have the portion of meat served to you at the table. Third, the only way you can increase your portion is at the expense of another — but that, as we shall see, is a dangerous path to pursue.

If we think of fate as determining the portion allotted to us, what exists within the outline of that portion constitutes our value and our identity — our whole life. Above all, for the Greeks, the portion allotted to us determines our honor. The possession of honor was the greatest treasure a person could have, and the more of it the better. The extent of our honor depends on the amount of the pie allotted to us. Bigger is better. As there is only so much to go around, we can only increase our honor at someone else's expense. The diagram becomes like a jigsaw puzzle, with each piece representing someone's amount of honor. For the Greeks, honor was all about position — getting a bigger piece of the pie. It is measured by what other people think of us. If we look good in the eyes of others, our honor has increased. If we look foolish or humiliated, instead of honor we receive shame. Soon it becomes like a competition, with the people watching deciding who has won. If someone steals a portion of honor from me, increasing their reputation or position by reducing mine, my only option is revenge. I must somehow take back that which was stolen from me, as my honor can only be increased by reducing the honor of another by a similar amount. This can only be done by taking action to reduce the dignity or value of the other person. Honor has nothing to do with ethics or morality. Even the gods were connivers and schemers, much like many of the Hindu gods, and were applauded for being so. Honor is simply becoming bigger than those around us.

The flip side of honor is shame. Shame is not guilt, as we understand it. It does not refer to a moral failure, something wrong we have done, an ethical standard we have failed to reach. Shame simply means being on the losing end of the power struggle. If a woman in ancient Greece was raped, she was shamed. Her honor was lost. She had done nothing wrong; indeed, she was the innocent victim. But now she is damaged goods, fit for no one to marry. Rape also represented the removal of a woman from her husband, taking with her his honor, as well as destroying hers. Likewise a crippled or deformed person is one with great shame, someone who is mocked and laughed at by others. Shame is external, an opinion others have of us which has nothing to do with the moral worth or value of the person. Shame is not like guilt, in that it cannot be forgiven. After all, the person shamed has not necessarily done anything wrong. Shame is therefore far more crushing than guilt. Guilt can be removed through forgiveness, but shame becomes a part of the essence of the person. It can only be diminished by taking revenge and, if the person is unable to do so, they must bear their shame forever.

Honor, the portion of the whole which is ours, is allotted or determined by fate. Ultimately, we cannot control what is happening to us. We may try, but ultimately we cannot move outside the amount of honor assigned to us. Even the gods have relative amounts of honor predetermined by fate and cannot move outside them. The whole universe is caught up in a gigantic given, something which simply is and cannot be changed. Human nature, however, pushes us toward the possession of as much honor as we can get. Going beyond the lines of the diagram, pushing the boundaries of fate, was what the Greeks termed transgression. Transgression does not express right or wrong in a moral sense; it means simply to challenge the boundaries fate has laid down for us. A person of noble character who transgresses the limits fate has established will be punished. But a scoundrel will prosper, provided he stays within his bounds, which may have been large enough for him to live a very pleasant life. After all, he might have been fated to attain wealth through cheating others. A second word beside transgression for challenging the boundaries was pride — *hubris*. *Hubris*, like transgression, does not express moral right or wrong, but simply trying to get more of the pie than fate has allotted us. *Hubris* and transgression upset the system, creating disorder. People begin to lose honor and must try to regain it from others. In the ensuing disorder, the weak and the innocent suffer, while the gods look on, enjoying the spectacle. Meanwhile, the terrifying beings called the Furies, whose job it is to enforce the lines of fate, strike the transgressors with dreadful punishments in their mission to restore order. They are assisted by Zeus, king of the gods, whose thunderbolts were aimed at those who dared to challenge fate. Yet in all this, even the fact we have transgressed is itself fated. There is no way out.

THE BIBLICAL REVOLUTION

It is an incredible fact that out of all religious viewpoints ancient and modern, only the Bible presents a way out of this diagram of fate. We appreciate this so little because we in the West enjoy the fruit of centuries of a Biblical understanding of reality, an understanding greatly under threat in our day. The Biblical revelation breaks the power of fate by presenting the truth of a supernatural, personal God who created everything out of nothing, before and outside of whom nothing exists or is "given," a God with unlimited freedom who created humanity in his own image. Early on in its pages, the Bible presents a triumphant picture of the God who destroys the bondage of fate. His children are imprisoned without hope under the cruel bondage of the greatest empire of the age. Through supernatural intervention, the cry of freedom goes up from the lips of Moses: "Let my people go!" By signs and wonders, God leads his people out of Egypt, breaking the power of fate and demonstrating that all of history is subject to his command. We are no longer imprisoned upon the line of time, or held in bondage within its ring or circle. We have the power to rise up above the line and break out of the circle through entering into personal relationship with this sovereign God. Freedom can be won by obeying God's law. The road out of Egypt is not the timeline of fate but the pathway to freedom. The way things are is not necessarily the way things have to be. A supernatural God gives us the ability to shape our lives and break free from what has bound us. At the Red Sea, the line of fate is both crossed and broken.

Christianity changes fate into destiny — a destination or eternal purpose we can reach to which the only real hindrance is our own obedience or disobedience. Nothing others can do to us, nothing fate can do, can prevent us from reaching the destiny God intends for us. Only our obedience or disobedience, by free choice, will determine the outcome.

To blame others, to become bitter at what others have done to us, to seek revenge, is to fall back into a fatalistic attitude. Fate is determined by uncontrollable outside forces, but destiny is something between ourselves and God alone. In this Biblical revolution was laid the entire basis of western science and civilization, which is built on the concept of progress, on the supposition that things can be changed, that they are not governed by fate or karma. It is why western Europe and North America have been historically different from fate-conditioned societies such as India. People can change things if they choose to make right choices.

But the Bible tells us more than this. Its message breaks the power of the honor and shame system. Honor no longer depends on how big we make ourselves at the expense of others. The Bible teaches that every person is of infinite worth and value. There is an unlimited amount of honor available, because honor, worth and value come from the infinite and unlimited God, who has chosen to pour out his love upon people without measure. True, the Bible teaches that all have fallen short of his standard and that this falling short represents transgression, a transgression which will prevent us from entering into our eternal inheritance. Yet this transgression is defined as guilt, not shame. Guilt is conscious deliberate wrongdoing against God and his law, entered into of our own free will. For this guilt there is a solution, a solution God himself has provided.

Consider the revolutionary implications of Philippians 2:6-11 in light of the Greek culture into which it was spoken. This passage tells us that Jesus, who held the place of highest honor — equality with God — did not seek to hold on to this place of honor. Rather, he did the following: he made himself of no reputation, took on the form of a slave (the lowest of the low), humbled himself and submitted to the shameful death of the worst kind of criminal. Yet God's Son did not lose any of his honor by doing so. The place of highest honor is now reserved for the very One who descended to the lowest place. The cross, the ultimate symbol to the Greek of shame and awful fate, becomes the very expression of God's mercy and forgiveness, and indeed of God's triumph. Once we have been forgiven, we can also humble ourselves in the service of others, forgiving them for how they have wronged us, knowing that our honor, far from being lost, will only be made all the more secure, and knowing also that the greatest honor consists in the deepest humility and service, for in this is reflected the very character of the God who is the source of all honor and bestows it so freely on people. When we are wronged, our honor is no longer at stake, because it no longer depends on what other people think of us or what fate assigns us. Instead, it depends only on the infinite worth and value God himself has placed upon us by the sacrifice of his Son.

Forgiveness and love represent the way of freedom. The vicious circle of shame and revenge is broken and replaced by the way of love. To the pagan mind, this was and is offensive. Friedrich Nietzsche, the nineteenth century philosopher who was the inspiration for Hitler, drew the same conclusions the Greeks did from the message of Christianity. To make love the greatest virtue is contemptible. To love your enemy, to honor those who are small and helpless, is nothing but a sign of weakness. A fate and honor system glorifies image, appearance and power. Might is right. Truth simply reflects the way things are, a world in which the strong are honored and the weak despised, for that is the fate allotted to them. When the moral values of Christianity are superficially intermixed with a pagan view of fate, it becomes only a short step to considering that somehow those with a small portion of honor actually deserve this for some wrong they have done, and that accordingly they should be punished. Nazism derived its essence via Nietzsche from the Greeks in adopting its policy of killing off the lame, the disabled, the unborn and the Jews. Some of these people (along now with the aged) we are still destroying, or would like to if we could.

Yet the Gospel declares that only in our weakness are God's strength and glory manifest. To the Greek congregation at Corinth still steeped in the thinking of fate and honor, Paul writes that their search for honor as kings misses the heart of a God who allows his greatest servants to carry the shame and dishonor of the world. His words build to a climax: "We have become a spectacle to the world... we are fools for Christ's sake... we are weak, but you are strong. You are held in honor, but we in disrepute [lit: without honor]" (1 Cor. 4:9-10). Such were words of horror to a pagan Greek. Yet in such shameful or earthenware vessels, in Paul's words to the same Corinthians, the Almighty Creator God shows forth his magnificence and glory (2 Cor. 4:7). In God's sight, those who are little are big and those who are big are little. As Jesus said, the first shall be last and the last shall be first. Only those coming as little children — the least significant and the weakest — can enter God's kingdom. But it is they who will enjoy the unlimited honor lavished upon them as sons and daughters of God.

THE RESURRECTION OF FATE

Christianity created a revolution which destroyed the pagan worldview of honor and fate. So why is this of interest to us today? For this reason: as western society has moved away from its Biblical foundations, the old ways of thinking have returned. In the final section of this chapter, let me describe the features of our contemporary culture and see how familiar it sounds.

MY RIGHTS OR YOUR RIGHTS?

The concept of rights has developed alongside the rejection of Biblical values. This seems a strange connection, but there is a valid reason for it. Genesis 1:28 teaches that humanity is made in the image of God. God establishes the value of the life of each person, such that Cain is held responsible for taking the life of his brother instead of protecting him. When we understand that the worth and value of each person are established by God, and that the depth of this worth is measured by the sacrifice of God's own Son, society is given a sufficient foundation to protect and value the life of each person. Not only that, but the Christian teaching concerning love and care for the poor and disadvantaged further ensures a just and compassionate society. What happens, however, when these foundations crumble? What happens when we begin to see humanity as the product of chance or evolution, rather than beings made in God's own image? Human nature being what it is, each person and ethnic or interest group rushes to secure their own rights, their own piece of the pie. As more and more people join the rush, inevitably some gain a bigger piece of the pie than others. Having a bigger piece makes them feel more significant, more secure, more important, more honored. Think for a minute of the current significance of the word "pride."

Some peoples' rights can only be enlarged at the expense of the rights of others. The woman has a right to an abortion, but the helpless infant loses the right to life. One racial or gender group, or social class, triumphs over another, until the loser seeks to take the ground back. In the absence of God, people turn to the courts, believing that laws can change human nature and ensure the expansion of their own particular rights. The LGBTQ community seeks greater honor by forcing others through legal action to assign to them rights to marry and adopt children, regardless of the consequences for the institution of marriage and the family. Feminists secure their goals by reducing the privileges of men, but then care little for the trans community, which responds by taking ground back the feminists have gained. Blacks, whites, Asians and aboriginals are pitted against one another. Unrest and confusion spreads as the lines of fate are upset. As more and more groups turn to the courts, power moves from elected representatives to the judiciary, from those who cannot afford the legal process to those who can. Once people have secured their own rights, most have little time to care for preservation of the rights of others. The end result of a focus on rights is that might becomes right. Just as it did in Russia in the 1920s, Germany in the 1930s, or China in the 1950s.

Does this all sound familiar? In the absence of Biblical foundations, within one generation our society has reverted to the fate and honor diagram of the pre-Christian world. Simply substitute honor for rights, and there you have it. Remember that pie and the slices of honor allotted to each? Remember the battle over enlarging my sphere at your expense? Remember the focus on my value being defined by what others think of me rather than on who God says I am? All we are lacking is the ancient Furies policing the lines and wreaking vengeance on those who transgress. But rest assured, though the Furies may not be at work, the demonic powers behind them most certainly are.

MY IMAGE OR GOD'S IMAGE?

If we understand the reality of God as the Bible presents it, and that we are made in his image, then the most important thing in life is God's view of us. Everything we have and are comes from him. The Bible teaches that he loves us so much that, in spite of our sin and rebellion, he gave his Son to die for us. Once society has lost the truth of the ultimate significance of what God thinks of us, something else must come in to fill the vacuum, and it does. What is now significant is not what God thinks of us, but what others think of us. Our worth and value are determined by the opinions of others, by how others see us. Is it any wonder that image has become everything in our culture? Image is all about making ourselves look good in the sight of others. Modern technology provides the means for us to be bombarded day and night with media messages about image. Our appearance is all about image. People will think better of us if we look younger, have a beautiful or handsome physique, have our face lifted, nose straightened, hair tinted and fat liposucted away. We are mesmerized by "reality" programs in which physically attractive men and women compete for greater honor in the eyes of the viewers, or others where unattractive men or women are shamed before national audiences by the pitiful comparison between their bodies and those of the buff and the beautiful. Identity is found in the virtual world of social media, in which no one knows anything about us except what we choose to present by electronic images. The economy is all about image. Fortunes are made by people trading electronic images called non-fungible tokens. We are persuaded that to own a certain vehicle, wear certain kinds of clothing or own various products will improve our image and cause people to think more highly of us. The power of advertising is greater than ever. Ask the shareholders of any social media company if you doubt me. That is where almost all their revenue derives from. Politics is all about image. Consider this contrast: on the one hand, Winston Churchill — short, fat, cigar-smoking, generally ill-tempered, rude and often depressed. On the other hand, today's politicians, who spend far more money on honing their media image than Churchill spent on his beloved daily bottle or two of champagne. Who was the greater leader? Yet Churchill would never have been elected today, because he would have lacked the image.

All you have to do is substitute the word "image" with "honor," and you can quickly see how completely we have returned to pre-Christian paganism. For the Greeks, the amount of honor we had was dependent entirely on what others thought of us. That is what we are increasingly left with today, as we turn our back on the truth of our eternal and infinite worth and value, a value placed upon us in all our human frailty by the Creator God of the universe. The Bible tells us we are made in his image, and that in the end, only his opinion of us counts. In our rebellion, we are determined to recreate ourselves in our own image, but this casts us into a prison where our worth and value are dependent on what others think of us, or how many social media followers we have, and that is a prison many will never break out of.

MY TRUTH OR YOUR TRUTH?

For two thousand years, we have seen the world around us from the perspective of God and his creation of the universe. There is meaning and purpose in life and in the world because God put it there. In recent years, however, we have been falling backward into a denial of the Biblical God and his status as personal Creator. Once this is gone, something else must step in to the vacuum. Since the days of Darwin, we have increasingly seen the universe as a product of impersonal evolutionary forces. In Darwin's day, this worldview could be uneasily combined with a traditional belief in God. But no longer. Today's science has taken on a life of its own. Science now claims to explain everything by its own laws, completely independent of God. The laws of physics are eternal. In the words of one scientist — and listen carefully to the significance of this phrase — "they just are." Humanity is nothing more than a collection of atoms, the product of strings of sugar and phosphate molecules known as DNA. What we are is predetermined by our genes. Yes, this does sound familiar. We are again caught in a fated prison. The universe, according to the latest theories in physics, is just as the Greeks thought it was, a giant eternally-existent inexplicable and meaningless given. We are a product of forces beyond our control, or even God's control. Eternal patterns of fate, in the form of the laws of physics and the way that certain molecules happened to fall into place when we were conceived, hold us captive. We are no longer accountable for what we do. After all, we had no choice — everything is genetically pre-determined.

When the Biblical God is no longer the author of life, and is replaced by the forces of fate, truth and meaning disappear as well. At best, truth becomes relativized. Truth is represented today by the way things are, as described by supposedly (but not really) objective scientific methods. There is no meaning or truth which explains how things got there in the first place, no truth which is bigger than the forces of fate as expressed in the laws of science. Each of us retreats to our portion of the pie, our piece of the jigsaw, to defend what truth, meaning or dignity we have left — in other words, to preserve our portion of honor. As we each defend our rights and protect our image, so also we each preserve our interpretation of truth. As there is no transcendent truth left, all we are left with is our own truth. According to this thinking, it doesn't matter at all whether my truth agrees with yours. What is important is that your truth cannot infringe on mine, because if it does, your honor is increased at my expense. I have the right to defend my truth and let it reign in my portion of the jigsaw. And there, in a nutshell, is a description of what we have come to call postmodernism. And behold the fury which falls on the brave soul who dares to declare that they have found a truth which is bigger than everyone's little piece, who dares to suggest that there is a transcendent objective standard of truth by which all peoples' understandings of truth will themselves be judged. Just as the Furies policed the lines of fate and punished those trying to climb out of their portion with terrible tortures, so the storm troopers of postmodernism hurl their thunderbolts at anyone trying to restore a standard of truth, particularly the one standard by which their entire system will fall, the self-revelation of the eternal God in his Biblical Word.

Things have in fact come full circle, for the present-day contrast between

Christianity and postmodernism can be summed up in no better way than it was two thousand years ago when Pontius Pilate shrugged his shoulders and said, "What is truth?" (Jn. 18:38), while Jesus Christ unapologetically declared these words which eventually saw him nailed to the cross: "I am the way, the truth and the life" (Jn. 14:6).

THE DAY THAT CHANGED HISTORY

In Acts 17, Luke records the story of Paul's mission to Athens. Athens was the intellectual and cultural center of the entire Roman Empire. Paul found himself first in the agora, where he stayed a while before he moved on. The agora was the commercial center of Athens — the marketplace. Where did he go after that, and why? He was standing in the shadow of the Acropolis, the great hill in the middle of the city that stood at the heart of Athenian history and religion. Temples and fortifications had been there for centuries, but a massive building program, begun under the great ruler Pericles in the fifth century BC, gave it the form it has to this day. Paul could have gone to the most sacred religious site on the Acropolis, the Parthenon, the temple of Athena the Virgin. Or he could have gone to the temple of Athena Nike, the goddess of war. Or he could have gone to the theater of Dionysus, the great sixth century BC theatre where all the great plays of antiquity had been staged. But he didn't go to any of them. He was aiming for somewhere else. He was not interested in challenging the commercial heart of the city (the agora), its religious center (the Parthenon), the heart of its great military (Athena Nike), or its cultural focus (the theater). The battle was not then and is not to this day over the economy, over religion, over military power, over politics, or over Broadway and Hollywood. Yes, there are battles raging over all of them, but Paul knew where the root of it all was.

And so he wound up at the Areopagus, the place at the foot of the Acropolis where the philosophers gathered to debate. He knew that in the end the battle was always in and for the mind, as he stated so powerfully in his second letter to the Corinthians. But there was something more than that. Athens was a city full of idol temples. As Paul pointed out, there was even a temple to the Unknown God, for the Athenians didn't want to miss any god out. All the gods were worshipped in multiple places. But oddly enough, at the Areopagus, the heart of the intellectual life of the city and the Empire, there was only one temple. And it was the only temple of its sort in all of Athens. It was the only place the Furies, those fearful beings who policed the lines of fate, were worshipped. On another day in Jerusalem, Jesus had gone to the Pool of Bethesda, where the sick were occasionally healed, and he went there for one reason — to shut it down. It wasn't needed any more. But on this day, Paul went to the Areopagus to shut down the temple of the Furies, along with the fate and honor system it represented. On that day, he initiated a great war which, several centuries later, brought the whole infrastructure of Greek religion down by the power of the Gospel. Those saved that day at the Areopagus were only the first fruits. And there, Paul kicked off a process by which the truth of Biblical revelation overcame the age-old power of fate.

The basis for Paul's message was found in the words of Jesus: "The truth shall make you free" (Jn. 8:32). Jesus drew the indispensable link between truth and freedom. When we lose truth, we lose freedom. The truth of the Gospel, of the Biblical message of God and his salvation, over the course of time set much of civilization free from the bondage of a lie which had engulfed the nations of the world in darkness. That lie, however, continued to rule in many cultures, even while it lay dormant in the West. But now it rises again, threatening to bring a new reign of darkness upon the earth. To withstand the enemy means first that we must understand his strategies. Then we must combat them — and the only way to do it is by uncompromised loyalty to the truth of God's Word. The tragedy is this: too often believers are found professing faith in Christ with their lips, while seeking at the same time to extend their rights, maintain their image, and preserve their own interpretation of truth, even cutting out those parts of the Bible they find offensive and consider no longer relevant.

If there was ever a time to fight for the uncompromised truth of God's Word, and the freedom from the power of fate it brings, it is now. God will hold us to account for what we do. To rise to this challenge, with all our mind, heart, strength and soul — this is our destiny.

TWO

THE COVENANT OF **FREEDOM**

THE WORD OF GOD AS A FOUNDATION OF FAITH

In chapter one, we talked about the importance of the Biblical revelation of the personal sovereign Creator God as the only basis for real human freedom. But on what basis are we to accept that revelation? The long history of liberal theology, or under its current label, "progressive" theology, has sought nothing more than to undermine confidence in Biblical revelation. As a consequence, churches and movements following that theology have died or are dying, because it leaves them nothing in which to believe. Archaeological and Biblical studies over the last century, however, have offered increasingly substantial evidence that the Bible is accurate. Progressive theology tends to rely on unreliable and speculative evidence which is often a century or more out of date. The true reason it rejects the Bible is because the Bible contradicts the secular philosophical basis of those who advocate it. It is far beyond the scope of this book to examine the kind of evidence I am referring to, though it is readily available in the work of many fine scholars. In this chapter, however, I can offer a foundation for the authority of that Biblical revelation. That is to say, I can present the claims the Bible makes for itself. And in these claims lie the only hope we have for finding and living in true freedom.

The ultimate foundation of our faith is God himself, revealed as Father, Son and Holy Spirit. But God has chosen to reveal himself in a very particular way, through his written Word, the Bible. All that we know about God finds its foundation in the Bible and must be tested by the Bible. In this way we can say that the Bible itself is a foundation of our faith. The Bible itself bears witness to its authority. The Psalmist declares: "Forever, O Lord, your word is firmly fixed in the heavens" (Ps. 119:89); and again: "Your word is a lamp to my feet and a light to my path" (Ps. 119:105). Jesus himself said: "Scripture cannot be broken" (Jn. 10:35). Paul wrote: "All Scripture is breathed out by God and is profitable for teaching, for reproof, for correction and for training in righteousness" (2 Tim. 3:16).

THE BIBLE AS COVENANT

The Bible is the self-revelation of God. God has given this revelation to us in a carefully-defined form which emphasizes its authority. This form is called a "covenant." While we can understand the essential nature of this covenant from the Bible itself, further light is thrown on it if we appreciate some of its historical background. God sent his Son in "the fullness of time" (Gal. 4:4), born in a day in which, more than ever before in history (thanks to the nature of the Roman Empire), the Gospel could easily be spread from one end of the civilized world to the other. In the same way, as Biblical scholars like Meredith Kline and others have shown, God chose to reveal himself first to a particular people at a particular place and time in history, and he did so for a reason. God fashioned his Word using the format of a treaty or covenant which all the peoples of that day and age would have understood.

HOW GOD USED THE ANCIENT CONCEPT OF TREATY OR COVENANT TO DEAL WITH THE ISRAELITES

Archaeological records show us that in the middle-eastern world of the second millennium BC (the time of Moses), conquering kings used a clearly-defined treaty format to impose their will on defeated peoples. This would have been the way the people of Israel understood for a people to come into submission to a king. The covenant (or treaty) God made with Moses and the children of Israel more or less exactly follows this format. God takes the place of the conquering king, and Israel are the people he conquers or asserts his rulership over. God used a vehicle for his revelation which would have been easily and clearly understood by all the people. Even though God's heart as a gracious king was not like the heart of earthly conquerors, nevertheless as king he expected allegiance from his people. At the very center of this treaty was God's sovereign action in answering the cry of Moses: "Let my people go!" This covenant is the basis of all our freedom. Without it, we are as much lost and in slavery as the children of Israel were in Egypt. God has come to set his people free.

The heart of this covenant (and of our Old Testament) is the Mosaic law, but it is not hard to see how the other parts of the Old Testament are related to it. Pre-mosaic history (Genesis) sets the stage for the delivery of the covenant by defining who God is and who his people are, as well as illuminating God's character and faithfulness. Post-mosaic history (the historical books) is a record of obedience or disobedience to the Mosaic covenant. The Psalms are largely the worship accompaniment to the covenant celebrations (whether daily or weekly rituals or the great festivals). The prophetic books contain God's warnings regarding disobedience to the covenant in subsequent times. The wisdom books (Proverbs, Ecclesiastes) bring practical application of the covenant to various areas of life.

The ancient treaty was a binding agreement between two parties, with copies to both. It came in written form, could not be abrogated or altered, and had promises and curses attached. This is the form the Mosaic covenant and the Old Testament take, and this is the foundation of their authority. The ancient treaty, once given, constituted a permanent, unchangeable legal document governing the relationship of the conquering king with the conquered people. Likewise, the Mosaic covenant (and, by extension, the entire Old Testament) was a permanent, unchangeable legal document detailing the requirements God placed upon his people. As with the ancient treaties, curses were attached to those who would alter the covenant document in any way (Deut. 4:2). To the Mosaic law were attached the historical narratives, Psalms, prophetic writings and wisdom literature, all of which were necessary elaborations of the covenant. The various parts of the Old Testament operate in unity to form God's ongoing conduct of his covenantal relationship with his people. Thus God himself fashioned the Old Testament as a permanently-binding and authoritative expression of his will, down to the last detail, even though he utilized humanly-understandable forms to express it. The ancient treaties show us exactly how the people of Israel would have easily comprehended the meaning of God's covenant as they received it, and why they held the Scriptures in such high reverence. This also explains why, even as other ancient treaties had to be preserved and guarded in a secure and often sacred location, the Mosaic covenant had to be preserved in the ark of the covenant. It explains why, following the treaty format, Moses wrote two copies of the covenant (Deut. 4:13, which has sometimes been misunderstood as one document written on two tablets), one for God and the other for Israel. Finally, it explains why the whole Old Testament was so meticulously passed down for well over a millennium in a society without printing presses! Covenant requires Scripture — where there is covenant, there will without doubt be a binding written record of its terms and conditions, and this is what the Bible is. You cannot have faith in the God of the Bible without possessing and obeying his written record of covenant. This is the foundation for our understanding of the authority of Scripture. The Bible is authoritative, therefore, not because the church says it is, but because God has inspired and created it himself, and it holds validity independent of any human agency or power.

This concept also explains the authority of the new covenant (or treaty) in Christ.

What about the New Testament? The New Testament is fundamentally a renewal of the Old Testament covenant. It is given by the same God, and its conditions are prophesied in the original covenant from Genesis all the way to Malachi. Moses, as well as Abraham and David, not to mention the prophets, spoke of the coming of the Messiah. The Old Testament, indeed, is in its entirety a prophetic foreshadowing of the New. The New Testament renews the Mosaic covenant, but alters its conditions, so that forgiveness comes by the blood of Christ rather than temple sacrifices. It also alters the nature of the covenant community, widening it from Jews to people of all nations. The structure of the New Testament is amazingly similar to that of the Old. At its heart is the giving of the covenant in Christ. Like the Old Testament, it has its history which sets the stage (Gospels), as well as a historical record of the subsequent obedience and disobedience of the covenant community (Acts and Epistles), gives prophetic insight and teaching (Epistles), wisdom (Epistles) and praise (Epistles and Revelation). This new covenant, being a renewal of the old, has the same characteristics of the latter, in that it comes from God, is inviolable and cannot be altered, and even has curses attached to that end (Rev. 22:18-19).

COVENANT AND CHURCH

Covenant creates a community or house of God which must live according to its commandments or suffer the consequences. The function of each testament or covenant is that of a legal document which defines the covenant community (Israel or the church) as a system of government by which the lordship of God through Jesus Christ is made real on the earth. Even as God through his creative word in Genesis fashioned the heavens and the earth, so God through his Biblical Word fashions the structure and nature of his covenant community upon the earth. As opposed to the Roman Catholic conception, in which the church creates the Bible and may therefore subject it to its own changing interpretation, we maintain that God through his Word stands as Lord over the church and calls the church into line with his Kingdom purposes. It is not that Scripture creates the church, but that God through Scripture orders the church and brings the church into submission to his will. Without Scripture, therefore, there is no way of knowing what the nature or will of God is other than through the limited and very clouded lens of revelation through creation, a revelation humanity has rejected (Rom. 1:18-32), and which brings no means of salvation from sin. It is Scripture which brings us the good news that a personal God who is sovereign over the universe has created each of us in his own image, and through the Gospel offers us true freedom.

God's old and new covenants were both made with his covenant people, not with isolated individuals. It is important to note, therefore, that the covenant extends now to the church, not just to Christians considered as individuals. Salvation can only be received on an individual basis, but it comes on the basis of the covenant God has made with his body, the church, and there is no true salvation outside of this Body of Christ. Those who seek to undermine the church or fail to recognize that it is the instrument of God's purposes on earth may find themselves outside the boundaries of his covenant and therefore lost forever. If we fail to build the church properly, we will survive, even though what we have built will not (1 Cor. 3:10-15). But if we seek to destroy the church, as some at Corinth were evidently doing, we will be utterly and eternally destroyed by God: "If anyone destroys God's temple, God will destroy him [lit: "tear him limb from limb"]. For God's temple is holy, and you [the Greek is plural] are that temple" (1 Cor. 3:17). Paul is using the concept of temple here to refer to the body of the church corporately, rather than (as he does in 1 Cor. 6:19) to refer to a person's individual physical body.

THE BIBLE'S LAST WORDS OF WARNING

As the Bible draws to a close, it presents us in Rev. 22:18-19 with a solemn warning. These verses stand in the same relation to the rest of Revelation (and, by extension, the New Testament as a whole) as do several almost identical passages in Deuteronomy to the Mosaic law:

"Listen to the statutes... you shall not add to the word that I command you... nor take away from it" (Deut. 4:1-2). "Everything I command you, you shall be careful to do. You shall not add to it or take away from it" (Deut. 12:32). For those who disobey: "The curses written in this book will settle upon him, and the Lord will blot out his name from under heaven" (Deut. 29:20).	"I warn everyone who hears the words of the prophecy of this book if anyone adds to them, God will add to him the plagues described in this book, and if anyone takes away from the words of the book of this prophecy, God will take away his share in the tree of life and in the holy city, which are described in this book" (Rev. 22:18-19).

Both Deuteronomy and Revelation deal with God's judgment on idolaters (Deut. 4:3; 12:30-31; Rev. 21:8, 27; 22:15). Both promise those who are obedient entrance into God's new land (Deut. 4:1; 12:28-29; Rev. 21:1-22:5). Both use "plagues" to describe the punishment for unfaithfulness (Deut. 29:21; Rev. 22:18). To add to or take away from the words of God's revelation, according to Deut. 4:3 and 12:29-31, means to accept the idea that idolatry is compatible with worship of the one true God. From the incident of the golden calf to that of the Baal of Peor, Israel faced the temptation to engage in idolatry, the worship of other gods. Reading the letters to the seven churches in Revelation (who are representative of the church through the ages) shows us that all of them, to one degree or another, faced the same pressure to compromise with idolatry. Idolatry is at the heart of compromise with Babylon, the beast and the false prophet. Professing Christians can thus dilute their commitment to worship God alone by adding to the teaching of Scriptures what is not in it, and by taking away from that teaching what is clearly there. To add to or take away from this revelation means to undermine the authority of God's Word. Those who thus undermine the authority of Scripture always and without exception do so in order to make way for worship of something other than God, whether that be a literal idol, or today's cultural or intellectual trends. Scripture offers a severe warning to those who suggest that the teachings of Scripture are culturally conditioned and no longer relevant for today, a suggestion which is nothing more than a cover for compromising with pagan and idolatrous cultural values.

As in the days of ancient Israel or the book of Revelation, these words of warning are particularly addressed to those who profess to be believers but are not. They are a warning not to the world, but to the professing church. At its beginning, Revelation shows itself to be a document written to believers: "Blessed is the one who reads aloud the words of this prophecy, and blessed are those who hear, and who keep what is written in it" (Rev. 1:3). The letter concludes by referring to "everyone who hears the words of the book of this prophecy" (Rev. 22:18). At its beginning and end, Revelation shows itself clearly to be a document written to believers, both genuine and merely professing. It is those within the visible, professing community of faith who hear and are warned in these closing verses of the Bible, and here is pictured most powerfully the fact that the battle is not from without, but from within.

This is why liberal or progressive theology has proven so destructive over the past two hundred years. Sadly, there are those within the visible church whose names are not written in the Lamb's book of life, and these are the very ones who attempt to draw the church off into idolatry. Of course, countless unbelievers who never made any profession of faith will also perish in the lake of fire, but these particular words of warning are directed to those who profess to be believers, but are not.

If we seek to build churches today on the solid foundation of God's unchanging word, those churches will remain standing on the rock of that foundation long after the changing tides and storms of human culture have abated. Against such churches the gates of hell — no matter how those gates appear, whether as opposing armies without or false prophets within — will not stand. Through such churches the message of freedom God gave first in Moses and then fulfilled in Christ will not be silenced. God give us the courage to build such churches in these days!

THREE

FREEDOM FROM THE **POWER OF SIN**

DEAD TO SIN BUT ALIVE TO GOD (ROM. 6: 1-14)

1What shall we say then? Are we to continue in sin that grace may abound?

The Jewish legalists were the greatest opponents of Paul's teaching on freedom. They and their followers within the church were constantly trying to bring believers back into some form of slavery. They were spiritually blind and could not understand Paul's teaching on grace. In fact, they were quick to distort it. In Rom. 3:5-8, Paul summarizes their argument: if it's true that, in spite of our sins, God still saved us, why then bother to live righteously at all? Of course, they didn't accept Paul's teaching that their good works were useless in God's sight. Good works cannot save us, the Gospel makes clear, for even our best efforts are fatally tainted by sin.

But Paul wants to make sure that his teaching cannot be interpreted as permission to carry on living the way we did before we became Christians. In Rom. 5:20, he had stated that where sin increased, grace increased all the more. So, he continues, shall we go on sinning in the assurance that God will go on forgiving us (Rom. 6:1)? He must answer the question decisively to clear up any wrong conclusions that might be drawn from his teaching. And he does so by showing that God both opposes sin and also gives us the power to overcome it.

In this discussion, he is operating on the assumption set out in words he had previously written in Gal. 2:18. There he states it is through the law that he died to the law and that if he returns to the law, he in fact is breaking the law and promoting sin. What he means is that the law has shown our sin for what it is, and revealed that none of us can truly keep the commands of God. The law has shown us that we are in fact slaves to the whole range of our sinful human desires. And the law, in bringing God's entirely justified judgment on our sin, pronounces the sentence of eternal slavery and death. But by sheer grace, through sending his own Son to die for us, God has saved us from his own law's just condemnation. And so if we return to the attempt to justify ourselves by what Paul calls "works of the law" (by which he means legalistic acts of self-righteousness), we are doing what the law never commanded us to do, and thus are breaking the law all over again.

God never intended that we should become righteous by keeping the law through our own unaided human efforts. He only ever had one plan for salvation, and that was through Christ. Scripture states this clearly and consistently, from its declaration concerning the triumph of the seed of the woman over the serpent in Gen. 3:15, through Abraham's declaration concerning the provision of a lamb (Gen. 22:8, 13-14), to the Mosaic law's prophetic foreshadowing of forgiveness through the sacrifice of animals, to Isaiah's suffering servant who was "pierced for our transgressions" (Isa. 53:5), and down to the very last chapter of the Old Testament, where it is prophesied that "the sun of righteousness shall rise with healing in its wings" (Mal. 4:2).

2 By no means! How can we who died to sin still live in it? 3 Do you not know that all of us who have been baptized into Christ Jesus were baptized into his death?

Paul now cuts to the heart of the matter. Is being saved by grace a license to sin? Not at all, he answers, for we have died to sin. But what does this "dying to sin" mean, and how does it relate to freedom? To understand Paul's discussion correctly, we must distinguish between three senses in which he refers to the Christian's death to sin. First, Christians have died to sin in God's sight once and for all through Christ's death on the cross. We have died and been raised up with Christ (Col. 3:1, 3). This first sense may be called the judicial sense, referring to God's legal judgment. God chooses to look at us now as he looks at Jesus. We are now totally free from the judgment that our sin brought upon us. The second sense of dying to sin is what we might call the moral sense. Every day the believer is called to live for Christ and turn his back on sin. Even though we have died and been raised with Christ (Col 3:1, 3), we are still exhorted to put to death daily our earthly sinful nature (Col. 3:5). This second form of dying to sin is a process, a battle in which we are still engaged, and will be as long as we live in this earthly life. In this sense, we are partially free from the hold of sin but still need the daily help of the Holy Spirit in a very real battle in which all of us are engaged. The third sense in which we die to sin we could call the eschatological sense. When we enter into Christ's eternal presence, we will be completely free from sin in every sense, judicial and moral. If through our salvation we have died to sin in God's sight, this must then be worked out in our present lives, and it will in turn surely lead on to perfect fellowship with Christ in eternity. Hence, if a person has confessed Christ and there is no subsequent change in their life, there is something seriously wrong, and they should examine whether they are truly converted. It can easily be seen that the first sense deals with the past, the second with the present, and the third with the future. We have been freed, we are being freed, and we will be freed. All three are true, but in different senses.

4 We were buried therefore with him by baptism into death, in order that, just as Christ was raised from the dead by the glory of the Father, we too might walk in newness of life. 5 For if we have been united with him in a death like his, we shall certainly be united with him in a resurrection like his. 6 We know that our old self was crucified with him in order that the body of sin might be brought to nothing, so that we would no longer be enslaved to sin. 7 For one who has died has been set free from sin. 8 Now if we have died with Christ, we believe that we will also live with him.

In verses 2-3, where we have died to sin by being baptized into Christ and his death, Paul is using the first sense, in which we are fully free from the judicial consequences of our sin. Baptism is an outward declaration of our decision of faith to find salvation in Christ. The life of the old person under the judgment of sin is now over, and a new life of freedom has begun. This is underlined in verse 4 by the fact Paul equates baptism with burial — that last and irrevocable sign, so often more powerfully moving than the funeral service, that the person deceased has truly died and that we must henceforth live without them.

But our judicial death, far from being the end of our battle, is in fact its real beginning. The goal of our baptism is that we might "walk in newness of life" (verse 4). Paul is now thinking of death and life not in the judicial sense, but in the moral sense. He is thinking not of our past decision of faith, but of our present life in Christ. What does he mean by "newness of life"? Greek has two words for "new." One *(neos)* refers to simple replacement of one thing with another, as in "a new pair of shoes." The other (kainos) refers to something of a totally different, even supernatural character, as in "God has given me a new life." The word in verse 4 is kainos. In the old life, we were subject to sin, but in this new life we have the power to fight against it. Our old man has been crucified (verse 6). This crucifixion is to be taken in a judicial sense. The whole old nature, the self in all its fallenness, has from God's perspective been put to death at the cross. Yet the old nature still exists in a moral sense, for believers are exhorted to put to death those things which are characteristic of it (see verse 13). The goal of this past judicial crucifixion is that we should no longer be slaves to sin in our present moral conduct. This is the meaning of verse 7: "For one who has died has been set free from sin." If we have died with Christ we can enjoy a new life of freedom from sin's power (verse 8).

9 We know that Christ, being raised from the dead, will never die again; death no longer has dominion over him. 10 For the death he died he died to sin, once for all, but the life he lives he lives to God. 11 So you also must consider yourselves dead to sin and alive to God in Christ Jesus.

Christ has been raised from the dead, and the hold of death has been broken over him, so that he enjoys true perfect communion now with God (verses 9-10). This one fact provides the secure basis of our own new life in Christ. From now on, we are to consider ourselves from God's perspective free from the power of sin and alive to him (verse 11). The command in verse 11 is in the present tense, implying a present, continuous, day by day lifestyle: "Keep on and on and on considering yourself dead to sin." Therefore, we must refuse to let sin reign in our mortal bodies ("bodies" standing for the whole of our human selves). We have died, yet we must continue to put to death all the things in our life which hinder Christ's character being formed in us. The battle for freedom is fought on a daily basis, but only by the power of the Spirit. Justification, in other words, is the only basis for sanctification. Everything rests on Christ's work for us on the cross, which releases the power of the Spirit into our lives. Hence sanctification is just as much by grace as justification. We must avoid the trap Christians often fall into of thinking of sanctification as something accomplished by our own hard work. We need the grace of God every day.

12 Let not sin therefore reign in your mortal body, to make you obey its passions. 13 Do not present your members to sin as instruments for unrighteousness, but present yourselves to God as those who have been brought from death to life, and your members to God as instruments for righteousness. 14 For sin will have no dominion over you, since you are not under law but under grace.

In verses 12-14, sin is pictured as a reigning monarch with troops at his disposal. But the power of this enslaver has been broken in Christ. Sin will no longer have lordship or authority over us (verse 14), for now we have freedom under the lordship of Christ. This does not mean that we are without sin. It means that now, for the first time, we have the ability to fight back against sin's power and begin to overcome it. We are under grace and not under law (verse 14). By this Paul does not mean that we are without law entirely, or that the law is completely abolished. Christ came to fulfill the law, not to abolish it (Mt. 5:17). What he means is that we are no longer under the law's just condemnation of our sin. We were prisoners of sin, but have now been set free in Christ. We'll see more of what this means in terms of our relationship to the law in the next chapter.

WHICH MASTER WILL WE SERVE? (ROM. 6:15-23)

15 What then? Are we to sin because we are not under law but under grace? By no means! 16 Do you not know that if you present yourselves to anyone as obedient slaves, you are slaves of the one whom you obey, either of sin, which leads to death, or of obedience, which leads to righteousness? 17 But thanks be to God, that you who were once slaves of sin have become obedient from the heart to the standard of teaching to which you were committed, 18 and, having been set free from sin, have become slaves of righteousness. 19 I am speaking in human terms, because of your natural limitations. For just as you once presented your members as slaves to impurity and to lawlessness leading to more lawlessness, so now present your members as slaves to righteousness leading to sanctification.

20 For when you were slaves of sin, you were free in regard to righteousness. 21 But what fruit were you getting at that time from the things of which you are now ashamed? For the end of those things is death. 22 But now that you have been set free from sin and have become slaves of God, the fruit you get leads to sanctification and its end, eternal life. 23 For the wages of sin is death, but the free gift of God is eternal life in Christ Jesus our Lord.

In these verses, Paul illustrates the meaning of freedom from sin using the example of human slavery. The only choice a person has is what they will be in slavery to — either righteousness leading to life, or sin leading to death (verse 16). There is no neutral position. This shows us that, contrary to the secular understanding of freedom, Christian freedom, which is the only true freedom, is not an end in itself. It can only be understood as freedom for something greater, which is laid out clearly here as slavery to righteousness and to God. If Christian freedom were an end in itself, ungoverned by any external constraints, it would imply that we are all capable of making selfless and Christlike choices in every situation. The fact is that in this present life we are not capable of that. Though we have received new life in Christ through the Spirit, we are still affected by the consequences of the fall. We live in what theologians call the "already-not yet." Contrary to the false charge of the Jewish legalists, Paul's understanding of grace does involve the daily decision to live a godly life. Jesus Christ has indeed set us free from slavery to sin and death, but the freedom he brings must be exercised in submission to his will for our lives, or it will be lost. We are not capable of finding our way on our own, without his law and his will to guide and guard us.

Once we are set free, we must not continue in sin (verses 15-16). If Christ is our Lord, he expects our obedience. It is impossible to continue in a sinful lifestyle and be a true follower of Christ. This is not legalism, for the ability to follow Christ comes only by grace. If we do not ask God for grace to live for him, we ought to question our profession of faith. Jesus was quite blunt: "By their fruit you will recognize them" (Mt. 7:16) — and no one could accuse Jesus of being a legalist! Where once we were slaves of sin, now we are slaves, not of Christ (as Paul might well have said), but of obedience (verse 16). The way he phrases this emphasizes just how strongly he wants to bring out the importance of obedience. Obedience, of course, is always obedience to Christ. And as verse 17 shows, obedience to Christ cannot be separated from obedience to the Scriptures, "the standard of teaching to which you were committed." You cannot be a believer and make up your own standards of conduct. You cannot alter, twist or delete parts of the Scriptures to justify your own sinful behavior. The phrase "the obedience of faith" stands like bookends at the beginning (1:5) and end (16:26) of Romans, and sets the context for the entire body of doctrine in between. The meaning of the Greek phrase is very simple: obedience is faith, and faith is obedience. They are inseparable.

The goal of Christian freedom is slavery to righteousness (verse 18). Paul needs to be so blunt because of the frailty of human nature, including that of believers: "I am speaking in human terms, because of your natural limitations" (verse 19). If we do not consider ourselves slaves of Christ, we will start to fall back into slavery to sin. We are not capable of living out our freedom in Christ independently, without either the empowering of the Spirit or the authoritative commands of Scripture which call us out of our own selfishness and into service to Christ. Contrary to the view of the world around us, freedom is not the highest goal to be sought, nor is it the greatest good.

Freedom, as Paul now illustrates, can be either positive or negative. When we were in slavery to sin, we were free from righteousness (verse 20). Yet that was not beneficial to us — in fact, the result of it was death (verse 21). But now, having been set free from the hold of sin, we now receive "fruit" or benefit which leads to sanctification (verse 22). While justification is immediate and instantaneous, sanctification is a lifelong process. Yet our newfound freedom can only be understood as a new but beneficial form of slavery, slavery to Christ. *Freedom never exists in a vacuum. It is always subject to a more powerful end, either sin and self, or God and his law.*

The "wages" which sin pays are death (verse 23). The Greek word "wages" refers to an allowance paid to his slaves by their owner. Sin pays a wage to those enslaved to it, and the wage is death. God, by contrast, pays no wage, for no one has ever earned it. Rather, he bestows eternal life as a "free gift." At the chapter's end, Paul has effectively answered the twisting of his teaching addressed at the beginning. Coming to Christ, far from encouraging sin, is the only true way of conquering it, and the only path to real freedom.

FOUR

FREEDOM FROM THE **LAW'S** CONDEMNATION

FREEDOM FROM LEGALISM (ROM. 7: 1-6)

Paul has just told believers they are no longer under the law, but under grace (Rom. 6:14). It is the fact we are not under law and have access to grace which gives us reason to believe we have real if not perfect freedom from the power of sin. If we are no longer under the law, we are freed from the law. But what does this actually mean? Paul takes all of chapter 7 to explain.

1Or do you not know, brothers—for I am speaking to those who know the law—that the law is binding on a person only as long as he lives? 2 For a married woman is bound by law to her husband while he lives, but if her husband dies she is released from the law of marriage. 3 Accordingly, she will be called an adulteress if she lives with another man while her husband is alive. But if her husband dies, she is free from that law, and if she marries another man she is not an adulteress. 4 Likewise, my brothers, you also have died to the law through the body of Christ, so that you may belong to another, to him who has been raised from the dead, in order that we may bear fruit for God.

Paul begins his explanation by appealing to the legal principle that the law has authority over a person only so long as they live (verse 1). His point is that the death of our old person in Christ brings about a decisive change in our relationship with the law. He illustrates this by an example from everyday life (verses 2-3). A married woman is bound to her husband only so long as he is alive, but if the husband dies, the woman is released to marry again. Finally, he draws a conclusion from the principle of verse 1: a death has occurred, and the believer, having being raised again to new life, belongs to Christ instead of the law (verse 4). The parallel to the marriage analogy isn't exact, or we would have expected our old "husband," the law, to have died, but the point is still valid. It takes a death to bring about a decisive change in human relationships.

It is in fact the believer who has died — or literally, "been put to death." The passive form of the verb emphasizes the fact it is God himself who has brought this death about. This is death in the legal sense, not the physical sense, for we remain physically alive throughout the process. But in God's sight, we are a new creation dead to our former life. This death sets us free from the power of sin, as chapter 6 has shown, but now Paul is about to show us it also sets us free from the power of the law. This has occurred "through the body of Christ," that is, through the death of Christ on the cross. The goal is that we might "belong to another." Here the thought of the marriage illustration has probably come back to Paul's mind, the thought being that we are now "married" to Christ. It also means we can "bear fruit for God." If we truly belong to Christ, the fruit of the Spirit (Gal. 5:22-23) will be evident in our lives.

5 For while we were living in the flesh, our sinful passions, aroused by the law, were at work in our members to bear fruit for death. 6 But now we are released from the law, having died to that which held us captive, so that we serve in the new way of the Spirit and not in the old way of the written code.

This new life of freedom from the law is very different from our old life. Before we were Christians, our "sinful passions, aroused by the law" led to death (verse 5). The clash between fallen humanity and the demands of God's law results in rebellion rising up within us, a rebellion that becomes all the more violent as the demands of God's law become clearer. Calvin said that the more the sin of humanity was held back by the restraints God put in place, the more it burst forth into greater fury. We can all testify that the tendency of a guilty conscience is to deny the truth in order to defend our own wrong choices. In the absence of any knowledge of God, the wrongness of our choices was real, but not so clear. But when we are confronted with the Biblical revelation of who God is and what he requires of us, we are faced with the reality of our continuous direct and willful disobedience. Our response to this is either denial (self-righteous legalism) or open revolt.

The law brings a judgment of condemnation on our rebellion. But when we come to Christ, we are "released from the law" (verse 5). Elsewhere Paul describes this as being "justified" (Rom. 3:24), a word borrowed from the law courts which means "acquitted." This is only possible because Christ took the punishment for our sin on the cross. God's holy anger against sin was poured out on his own beloved Son. The judgment of the law which once condemned us is now cancelled. We are set free from a judgment which would have resulted in an eternity without God. But this freedom has a definite purpose. It is never *freedom from* without being *freedom for.* We are set free "to serve in the new way of the Spirit and not in the old way of the written code [lit: letter]" (verse 6). The Holy Spirit is revealed as the agent who makes this freedom and new life possible.

What does Paul mean by freedom from the old way of the "written code" or "letter"? It can't be simply that the law is abolished, because Jesus said he did not come to abolish the law but to fulfil it (Mt. 5:17). Paul said himself earlier in Romans that the gospel, far from overthrowing the law, actually establishes it (Rom. 3:31). The law is not opposed to the promises of God (Gal. 3:21). Neither is the law opposed to the Spirit, for the law is "spiritual" (Rom. 7:14). In fact, it is the Spirit who enables a true fulfilment of the law (Rom. 8:4). Paul must mean something different here. He does not refer to the *old way of the law*, but the *old way of the "letter"* (the Greek word is gramma). To see the law only as "letter" refers to the legalistic misuse or misunderstanding of the law Paul has condemned in the Jewish teachers of Romans 2, who professed to uphold the law even while they were breaking it. They reduced the law to the performance of certain outward rituals, and lost sight of its true meaning and the depth of its demands. Jesus condemned the same attitude at length in the Sermon on the Mount. The way of *gramma* is the way of self-righteous observation of external rituals, while ignoring the law's true meaning and requirement. Legalism operates by reducing the law to the performing of certain superficial actions. In Paul's day, that meant things like circumcision, ritual washings, various dietary practices and so on. The Pharisees could fulfil those requirements and feel they had earned their own righteousness in the sight of God. They were offended by Jesus' suggestion that they were the blind leading the blind. We can fall into the same danger. Christians have sometimes reduced the gospel to the keeping of certain practices such as abstaining from alcohol, smoking or dancing, avoiding movie theaters, even playing cards. There may have been good reason for some of these prohibitions, but when they become the primary measurement of holiness, we are in big trouble, for people can keep these rules while having no heart knowledge of God at all.

So what Paul is pronouncing here is *not the end of the law, but the end of legalism.* The gospel exposes all forms of rebellion, including legalism. The good news is that the just condemnation God pronounces on this rebellion is removed through the cross. We are set free from slavery to sin, we are set free from God's judgment, and we are even set free from the legalistic pressure to make ourselves holy in God's sight.

THE LAW IS NOT THE BARRIER TO FREEDOM (VERSES 7-25)

Is there something inherently wrong with the law which causes God to set us free from all relationship with it? This is often the way the gospel has been presented, and this has caused no end of problems in trying to understand and practice Christian freedom. It has also placed a great divide between the Old and New Testaments, which obscures the fact that the two are integrally related. The new covenant, as noted in chapter two, is at its heart a renewal of the old covenant. As Augustine said fifteen hundred years ago, the New Testament is hidden in the Old, and the Old Testament is revealed in the New. *The question of the role of the law and its fulfillment in Christ is central to a proper understanding of the relationship of the two covenants.* And if the new covenant brings freedom, it is critical to gain a correct understanding of freedom in relation to the law.

According to Rom. 5:20, the law "came in to increase the trespass." In 6:14, Paul made the further assertion that sin's hold on us is broken because we are no longer under the law. So is the law itself somehow evil? Paul has to make sure no one draws that conclusion from what he has said, and that is what the rest of chapter 7 is about. It is divided into three paragraphs. In the first (verses 7-12), Paul argues that the law is good, but that sin has used it for its own wicked purposes. In the second (verses 13-23), he argues that it is sin, not the law, which is responsible for humanity's spiritual death. The final paragraph (verses 24-25) sums up the true nature of the conflict in the Christian life, and how the law fits into that. And this

in turn directly paves the way for Paul's teaching on freedom, the Spirit
and the law in chapter 8.

*7 What then shall we say? That the law is sin? By no means! Yet if it had
not been for the law, I would not have known sin. For I would not have
known what it is to covet if the law had not said, "You shall not covet."
8 But sin, seizing an opportunity through the commandment, produced
in me all kinds of covetousness. For apart from the law, sin lies dead. 9 I
was once alive apart from the law, but when the commandment came,
sin came alive and I died. 10 The very commandment that promised life
proved to be death to me. 11 For sin, seizing an opportunity through the
commandment, deceived me and through it killed me. 12 So the law is
holy, and the commandment is holy and righteous and good.*

Let's look at the opening paragraph first. A noteworthy feature of the
entire chapter is the way in which Paul speaks in the first person singular.
In the first paragraph and slightly overlapping into the second (verses
7-13), he speaks in the past tense, whereas in the rest of the chapter, he
speaks in the present. But who is he speaking about? Is he speaking about
himself or someone else? In verse 9, he says that once he lived without the
law. That couldn't possibly be Paul describing his own personal experience,
for he was raised in the strictest practice of the law, "circumcised on the
eighth day, of the people of Israel, of the tribe of Benjamin, a Hebrew of
Hebrews; as to the law, a Pharisee" (Phil. 3:5). The clue to the correct
meaning lies in allusions he makes in the text to the story of the fall. The
paragraph borrows terminology from the Genesis story to retell the story
of Adam and Eve falling prey to the serpent. Sin (the serpent) seized an
opportunity through the commandment (not to eat of the tree), deceived
me (as the serpent deceived Eve) and killed me (verse 11). Paul uses the
first person because he has just finished teaching that all of us fell in Adam
(5:12-21). And he goes on to connect God's commandment to Adam
with the law later given to Moses (5:14). Because all of us are personally

involved, Paul can speak as a representative of fallen humanity.

But if Paul is alluding to the fall, why then does he say: "For I would not have known what it is to covet if the law had not said, 'You shall not covet'" (verse 7). God said nothing to Adam about not coveting. Or did he? The commandment "Do not covet" was closely linked by Jewish teachers to the story of the fall, because of Eve's illegal desire for the forbidden fruit. The act of coveting was seen as summing up the whole expression of our sinfulness and rebellion against God in the garden. Sin found an opportunity in the commandment given in the garden not to eat the forbidden fruit. Through our disobedience, sin then was then able to produce all kinds of covetousness in us (verse 8). Paul was following his Rabbinic teachers in interpreting the sin of Eve as coveting.

This is confirmed when we look further at verse 9. Paul again alludes to the account of Adam in the garden: "I was once alive apart from the law, but when the commandment came, sin came alive and I died." Only Adam could truly be said to have been fully "alive" before giving way to sin, because sin first entered when Adam disobeyed the commandment. Then later, sin was clearly defined and multiplied through the law, as 5:20-21 makes clear. *Paul is using the Genesis story to try to illustrate how sin uses a direct commandment, first with Adam and then later with the law, to increase its power over humanity.*

The commandment, which God intended to bring life, actually brought death (verse 10). Sin deceived me and, through the commandment, put me to death. Here is another clear reference to Genesis, for the verb "deceived" alludes to the action of the serpent in regard to Eve (Gen. 3:13). The commandment, which came from the mouth of God himself, was not to blame. Neither, says Paul, can we say that the law (which equally came from God) is to blame, and this is the bigger point he wants to make.

Everything that could be said of the commandment to Adam can also be said of the law. The enemy uses the good commands of the law to distort the purposes of God, to question his goodness and to tempt us to rebel against him. Sin even so distorts the command as to make people believe they can fulfill it by their own righteousness. Yet the law itself is not to blame. Far from it, Paul concludes: "The law is holy, and the commandment is holy and righteous and good" (verse 12). We could take this a step further by saying that neither is the gospel to blame for the fact that it also is used by the enemy to incite rebellion in fallen humanity, indeed a greater rebellion, for this rebellion culminated in the crucifixion of the Son of God, and continues today wherever in the world the crucified Savior is rejected and his followers are persecuted or killed.

These words of Biblical scholar Charles Cranfield in his commentary on Romans catch Paul's meaning exactly: *"The commandment was a merciful limitation on man designed to protect him and preserve his true freedom and dignity, yet in the garden it was misinterpreted by man as a taking away of his freedom to do what he wished and as an attack on his worth and value as an independent being, and thus became the occasion for his rebellion and anger against God. Sin uses the rebellion thus aroused to provoke man to ever-increasing acts of covetousness, thus increasing his disobedience to God."* God's command, which superficially limits our freedom, in truth keeps it safe. Fallen human nature saw God's command only as limiting the freedom it wanted, yet in our rebellion we sealed our sentence of slavery to sin and death. This understanding of freedom in relation to the commandments of God is critical for us to grasp today if we are to enter into the full freedom we have in Christ.

13 Did that which is good, then, bring death to me? By no means! It was sin, producing death in me through what is good, in order that sin might be shown to be sin, and through the commandment might become sinful beyond measure. 14 For we know that the law is spiritual, but I am of the flesh, sold under sin. 15 For I do not understand my own actions. For I do not do what I want, but I do the very thing I hate.

The first paragraph has shown that the law is good, but has been used by the enemy for his own evil purposes (verses 7-12). The second paragraph (verses 13-23) explains that it is sin, not the law, which leads to spiritual death. The first question, "Is the law sin?," having been answered in the negative, Paul now proceeds to a second question: "Did that which is good, then, bring death to me?" (verse 13). As in verse 7, the answer is clear: "God forbid!" The truth is that sin made use of a good thing (the law) in order to bring about death. Contained within the second half of verse 13 are two clauses of purpose ("in order that"), both of which express a part of God's purpose in giving the law. He gave the law *in order that* sin might be recognized as sin, and *in order that* through the law sin might become utterly sinful. The law first uncovers the true reality of sin. Then, by challenging our rebellion, the law causes sin to be "increased" (become utterly sinful) in the hearts of those who rebel (5:20). *This does not express the entire purpose of God in giving the law,* as we shall see in chapter 8. The gospel has a similar but even greater effect than the law, in that through the gospel events the sin of humanity was so uncovered and enhanced that it led to the rejection and death of God's own Son. Wherever in the world the gospel is preached, it often has the same effect. This was indeed part of the purpose of God in regard to the gospel, but clearly not the entire or even the main purpose. The same is true of the law.

In verse 14, Paul switches abruptly from the past tense to the present. Having described the events of the past in regard to the fall and the giving of the law, he now appears to be describing how these events are working themselves out in the present. We may ask the question we did earlier with regard to the statements in verses 7-13, "Of whom is Paul speaking?" He cannot be speaking of *himself prior to conversion.* That would not account for the continuous use of the present tense. But beyond that, Paul's own past as a self-righteous Pharisee, apparently blameless before God, as recorded in Phil 3:6, is far removed from the picture here of a man deeply conscious of his own sinfulness. Neither, for the same reason, could he be speaking of *himself as representative of non-Christian Jews in general,* for Paul has presented them in chapter 2 as people certain of their own righteousness. And he could not be speaking of himself as representative of humankind in general as he was in verses 7-13, for this would be completely at odds with his presentation in 1:18-32 of humanity's fallen state and complete disregard for the ways of God. There is only one possibility left. *He must, therefore, be speaking of himself as a representative of the present experience of believers.* This is in line with the fact that chapters 1-3 speak of the life of unbelievers, while chapters 5-8 describe the Christian life. The fact that Paul describes his own experience this way underlines both the ongoing battle against sin, and our desperate daily need for the power of the Holy Spirit to honor God and his commandments in our lives.

The law is "spiritual" (verse 14), meaning both that it comes from God and that it can only be properly understood with the help of the Holy Spirit (2 Cor. 3:1-17). Those without the Spirit understand the law only as "letter" (7:6). The law is spiritual, but I am sinful, "sold under sin." How could Paul describe himself or any other believer in such terms? Two reasons present themselves. First, the Gospel, even more than the law, shows up the seriousness of my sin, and how far I am from the standard of God's holiness. The closer we get to God, as godly Christians have testified through the ages, the more hopeless we realize our situation is without God's grace, and the more awful appears our sin and rebellion. Even our finest deeds now seem indeed like Isaiah's filthy rags (Isa. 64:6). Second, Paul's description here must be taken alongside what he is going to say in chapter 8, for the two chapters hang closely together. The struggle of believers against sin and our overcoming by grace through the empowering of the Holy Spirit are both real aspects of the Christian life. Concentrating solely on the struggle against sin would lead us to despair, but focusing only on overcoming by the Spirit would result in pride and a false sense of security. Both aspects must be taken together, for the Christian life is lived in tension between the "already" and the "not yet." As Paul has stated in chapter 6, we do have power to fight back against sin, but we can never underestimate the ways in which we can still give way to the enemy and fall into disobedience to God.

The next verses, starting with "For I do not understand," explain what it means to be "sold under sin." Paul begins by stating that he does not "know what he does" (verse 15) — yet in fact he is clearly aware of his actions. The difficulty is easily resolved. The verb is better translated "I do not acknowledge" or "I do not approve of" what I do. The same verb is used in Greek of a father "acknowledging" a child as his own. Here is the inner conflict of the believer to which all of us we can bear witness. We do things we do not approve of. In fact, Paul continues, "what I do I hate." While an unbeliever might have some occasional regret over their actions, it is unlikely, if they were otherwise in sound mind, that they would be pictured as hating their own moral choices and acts. But if the individual pictured here knows God and is indwelled by the Holy Spirit, has a deep consciousness of the chasm between God's righteousness and their own sinfulness, and is crying out to God for help in the battle against sin, the words spoken in verse 15 are entirely appropriate. They are appropriate because they acknowledge both a genuine desire to obey God's law, yet an understanding of how far short we fall. In 3:23, Paul says that all have sinned (past tense), and that all *continue to fall short* (present tense). The hatred of sin pictured in verse 15 can only come from the Holy Spirit who indwells us.

16 Now if I do what I do not want, I agree with the law, that it is good. 17 So now it is no longer I who do it, but sin that dwells within me. 18 For I know that nothing good dwells in me, that is, in my flesh. For I have the desire to do what is right, but not the ability to carry it out. 19 For I do not do the good I want, but the evil I do not want is what I keep on doing. 20 Now if I do what I do not want, it is no longer I who do it, but sin that dwells within me.

The second paragraph continues. In verse 16, Paul says that his failure to meet God's standard the way he wants to shows that he agrees with the law that it is good. Only Christian believers truly align themselves with God's law. The Gentile unbeliever would not acknowledge the law at all. The Jewish unbeliever, while acknowledging the law, would not agree that the law itself shows up the darkest recesses of sin in their heart. It is because the conflict pictured in verse 16 is a reality in the believer's life that Paul can say in verse 17 that it is "no longer I that do it, but sin that dwells within me." Paul is not excusing himself. After all, he has spent the first three chapters of the letter spelling out how all people are completely responsible for their sin. Rather, he is acknowledging the extent to which sin exercises control over his life. Again, of course, this must be held in balance with the wider understanding in chapters 6 and 8 that the control sin exercises now is not the unstoppable power it previously was. Verse 18 shows that what is said in verse 17 is not meant to excuse us, for it throws the problem back onto ourselves: nothing good dwells within my flesh, meaning my whole fallen human nature, or what is in me apart from the working of the Holy Spirit. Paul continues: "I have the desire to do what is right, but not the ability to carry it out." He does not mean he cannot do anything at all, but that whatever he does never fully accomplishes what he desires. He sees the perfect will of God, but cannot reach it. Only believers could have such an ache in their hearts to perform the Father's will. Then verses 19-20 repeat the substance of verses 15-17.

21 So I find it to be a law that when I want to do right, evil lies close at hand. 22 For I delight in the law of God, in my inner being, 23 but I see in my members another law waging war against the law of my mind and making me captive to the law of sin that dwells in my members.

The second paragraph approaches its end. In verse 21, Paul begins to draw some conclusions from the preceding verses. The verb "find" (Greek *heurisko*) means to "prove for oneself by experience." Paul is saying that his experience proves that when he turns to do the good, sin stands in the way. Yet he goes on to say he delights in God's law (verse 22). To delight in the law is surely the cry of the sincere believer. This rejoicing occurs in the "inner being." This is that deep place in the believer's heart where the Holy Spirit works, as shown by Paul's prayer that "… he may grant you to be strengthened with power through his Spirit in your inner being" (Eph. 3:16). The sentence is concluded in verse 23: "…but I see in my members another law waging war against the law of my mind and making me captive to the law of sin that dwells in my members." In verses 22-23, two laws are pictured, at war with each other. The "law of sin" is waging war against the "law of my mind." The first law represents the power or control exercised over us by sin. The "law of my mind" is the the "law of God" spoken of in verse 22. Is it possible that such a war could occur within the life of the Spirit-filled believer? The answer must surely be yes. Indeed, it is only within the believer that the war is waged. There is no such battle going on in the unbeliever, who does not even acknowledge God's law or claim on his life. But within the believer the battle has been joined (Rom. 6:12). The battle is fierce, but the eventual outcome, as chapter 8 shows us, is not in doubt.

24 Wretched man that I am! Who will deliver me from this body of death? 25 Thanks be to God through Jesus Christ our Lord! So then, I myself serve the law of God with my mind, but with my flesh I serve the law of sin.

Verses 24-25 form a conclusion to all that Paul has said in verses 7-23. The speaker cries out: "Wretched man that I am! Who will deliver me from this body of death?" "Wretched" refers to genuine distress or anguish, but it does not necessarily imply hopelessness. The question Paul cries out is rhetorical in nature: he knows what the answer is, and that his hope in Christ is secure. In fact, he indirectly answers his own question in the very next phrase: "Thanks be to God through Jesus Christ our Lord!" (verse 25a). Verses 14-25a as a whole are then summed up in verse 25b: "So then, I myself serve the law of God with my mind, but with my flesh I serve the law of sin." In the same person, two things play out: a measure of obedience to the law of God and a measure of obedience to the law or power of sin. In the mind or inner person, where the Holy Spirit is at work, there are the beginnings of a genuine obedience to God's law. Yet in the flesh (the fallen human nature that is still a reality), the power of sin is operating. Only in the Christian believer could both realities exist at the same time. Through his use of the first person singular and the present tense, Paul is expressing in these verses both the struggle that he faces personally in his own battle against sin, and the struggle he knows is real in the heart of every believer. To ignore or deny the existence of such a struggle betrays a deception as to the measure of our own sanctification, or even perhaps the presence of a legalistic spirit.

The battle for freedom is fought on the basis of the work of Christ. The outcome of the battle is certain. Yet in the meantime the battle persists, and can only be fought by the empowering of the Spirit. Toward the end of the second world war, allied forces landed in Normandy, an event known as D-day. The war did not end until V-day, almost a year later. Many battles were fought and many casualties occurred between those two days. But from D-day onward, the outcome was determined. We live between the D-day of Jesus' resurrection and the V-day of his final return. There are battles to fight, many of which will not be easy, yet the outcome is assured. And so even in the midst of battle, we can join with Paul in looking forward confidently to the deliverance awaiting us in Christ, and with him declare: "Thanks be to God through Jesus Christ our Lord!"

FIVE

FREEDOM AND
NEW LIFE IN THE SPIRIT

One key word defines Romans 8 — *pneuma.* This word is used 34 times in Romans, and 21 of these occur in chapter 8. *Pneuma* can refer either to the Holy Spirit or the human spirit. All but two of the 21 occurrences in chapter 8 refer to the Holy Spirit. The theme of chapter 8 is the meaning of freedom in Christ through the Holy Spirit.

Romans 6-8, taken together, give us the entire theological basis of Christian freedom. It is freedom from the power of sin (chapter 6), freedom from the just condemnation of the law (chapter 7), and freedom to live a righteous life in the power of the Holy Spirit (chapter 8). As the chapter unfolds, we will see what this freedom the Holy Spirit gives us looks like.

FREEDOM COMES THROUGH THE HOLY SPIRIT (VERSES 1-11)

1There is therefore now no condemnation for those who are in Christ Jesus. 2 For the law of the Spirit of life has set you free in Christ Jesus from the law of sin and death.

Paul previously made the statement that we are released from the law to serve God "in the new way of the Spirit" (7:6). After a digression on the relationship of sin, self and the law (verses 7-25), he now takes up the theme of new life in the Spirit.

The law no longer brings condemnation (verse 1) because "the law of the Spirit of life" has set us free from "the law of sin and death" (verse 2). The law of sin and death represents the power or control of sin, and the law of the Spirit of life represents the power and working of the Holy Spirit. God's gift of the Spirit has set us free from the hold of sin. The believer still battles against sin, as chapters 6 and 7 have shown, yet not in the same way as the unbeliever does. Believers serve God in their inner person (7:22), and wage war against the dominion of sin (7:23). The new element in chapter 8 is that the key to victory in this battle is the empowering of the Spirit. This victory will find complete fulfillment at the Lord's return (8:23). Though we struggle now, we know that we are on the winning side.

3 For God has done what the law, weakened by the flesh, could not do. By sending his own Son in the likeness of sinful flesh and for sin, he condemned sin in the flesh, 4 in order that the righteous requirement of the law might be fulfilled in us, who walk not according to the flesh but according to the Spirit.

How this works is further explained in verses 3-4. God has done what "the law, weakened by the flesh, could not do." Our problem lay in the flesh, not the law, yet the law had no power to help us overcome it. But God sent his Son "in the likeness of sinful flesh and for sin." The phrase "in the likeness of" draws a distinction between the way in which Christ took on our flesh, and the way in which we ourselves live in that flesh.

Though Christ fully assumed our humanity, he did so in such a way that he never became sinful as we are. Christ's humanity was real, however, for the very next statement refers to God's judging sin "in the flesh," meaning in the flesh of Jesus. Jesus was in the flesh like us, "yet without sin" (Heb. 4:15). That God sent his Son "for sin" means he sent Jesus *in order to deal with sin* by destroying its power. By sending Christ for sin, God "condemned sin in the flesh." For God to condemn sin must mean something more than simply passing judgment on it. The law was perfectly able to do just that, yet here Paul says God did something which *was impossible for the law to do.* Hence, the judging of sin must be not only the *passing of sentence* upon sin, but also the *carrying out of that sentence* by the destruction of the power of sin itself. The phrase "in the flesh" tells us where God's judgment fell — on the flesh of Jesus Christ, upon whom fell all the anger of God against all the sins of humanity ever committed. Without the exercise of the wrath of God against his own sinless Son, there can be no true forgiveness of sins, regardless of what some contemporary theologians suggest. A careful study of the meaning of the word "propitiation" (Greek *hilasterion*) in 3:25 ("whom God put forward as a propitiation by his blood") will verify this assertion. If the wrath of God was not visited upon Christ at the cross, the question arises why Christ needed to die at all.

Thus far it is clear that God sent his Son in order that we might gain freedom from the power of sin through the work of the Holy Spirit. But what is the purpose of this freedom? Freedom, as we have seen, is not just freedom *from*, it is freedom *for.* At the beginning of verse 4, the words "in order that" indicate the goal God has in mind. His purpose is "in order that the righteous requirement of the law might be fulfilled in us, who walk not according to the flesh but according to the Spirit." *This verse states the very meaning of Christian freedom.* The phrase "righteous requirement" correctly translates the Greek word *dikaioma* as singular, not plural. This highlights the fact that the law's requirements are a unity, "a recognizable and intelligible whole, the fatherly will of God for his children" (Charles Cranfield).

This shows us that the statement here that the righteous requirement of the law is fulfilled in love does not represent a reduction of the law, as if now all we have to do is "love," for that leaves "love" completely (and dangerously) undefined. What it shows is that the *one thread of love runs through all the commands* of the Old Testament law. This causes them to be seen as expressing the *one righteous requirement of God for his children.* Whether it be the command not to covet, the command to care for widows and orphans, or the command not to move a neighbor's boundary stone, the one thread of love runs throughout. Paul is interpreting Jesus (Mk. 12:28-34), who understood that the law in all its dimensions could be expressed as commanding love for God (Deut. 6:4-5) and love for neighbor (Lev. 19:18). He takes up this theme again in 13:8-10, where he speaks of the "summing up" of the law in the command to love (explained in more detail in chapter six).

God's goal in sending Christ to free us from the power of sin was that his law would be truly established. In this, we see the fulfillment of the prophetic promises of the Old Testament. God promises to write his law on peoples' hearts (Jer. 31:33). He will put his Spirit within them, so that they will walk in his statutes (Ezek. 36:26-27). As Jesus said, through him the law will be fulfilled, not abolished (Mt. 5:17). The Pharisees had twisted obedience to the law into a series of spiritually meaningless self-righteous accomplishments by which they attempted to make a claim upon God. They reduced the requirements of the law and then claimed they had fulfilled it. But here Paul shows us that the law is truly fulfilled only in those who walk "according to the Spirit."

For the first time, believers are enabled, by the power of the Spirit, to turn their hearts toward God in such a way that his law can be said to be fulfilled in their lives. What was glimpsed in the Old Testament, and seen from time to time in the lives of people like Abraham, Sarah, Esther and David, has now become the norm for new covenant believers upon whom the Holy Spirit has been outpoured. Augustine put it this way: *the law was given that grace might be sought; grace was given that the law might be fulfilled.* We are not justified by keeping the law. But we must be justified in order to keep the law. Paul says the same thing elsewhere: "For by grace you have been saved... not a result of works... For we are his workmanship, created in Christ Jesus for good works..." (Eph. 2:8-10). It is precisely because we have been saved by grace that we now can perform good works, not in a legalistic fashion, but by the power of the Spirit and to the glory of God. This empowers us to serve Christ, and to serve Christ and enjoy the blessing of his presence is surely the highest form of freedom we can attain on earth.

5 For those who live according to the flesh set their minds on the things of the flesh, but those who live according to the Spirit set their minds on the things of the Spirit. 6 For to set the mind on the flesh is death, but to set the mind on the Spirit is life and peace. 7 For the mind that is set on the flesh is hostile to God, for it does not submit to God's law; indeed, it cannot. 8 Those who are in the flesh cannot please God.

The next verses provide a further description of what it means to fulfill the law by walking according to the Spirit. There are two choices: to take the side of the flesh or to take the side of the Spirit. We are in a life-and-death battle, and in this battle there is no neutral ground (verse 5). To set the mind on the flesh is death, but to set the mind on the Spirit is life and peace (verse 6). On the one side is slavery to sin, on the other slavery to God, which is true freedom. Christians are by no means perfect, but they have chosen to keep their lives consistently rooted and grounded in

God. The mind of the flesh, on the other hand, is hostile to God, and this hostility is identified by its refusal to submit to God's law (verse 7). Those walking in the flesh cannot please God (verse 8). If we are not enlisted in the service of Christ, we are working on the side of the enemy, whether we know it or not.

9 You, however, are not in the flesh but in the Spirit, if in fact the Spirit of God dwells in you. Anyone who does not have the Spirit of Christ does not belong to him. 10 But if Christ is in you, although the body is dead because of sin, the Spirit is life because of righteousness. 11 If the Spirit of him who raised Jesus from the dead dwells in you, he who raised Christ Jesus from the dead will also give life to your mortal bodies through his Spirit who dwells in you.

Every believer in Christ is indwelled by the Spirit — not just those who possess certain spiritual gifts. If we do not have the Spirit within us, we are not Christians at all (verse 9). And where the Spirit is, there is freedom (2 Cor. 3:17). If Christ is in us, then "although the body is dead because of sin, yet the Spirit is life because of righteousness" (verse 10). The Christian must still submit to death as part of the wages of sin, because that is the result of the curse on our fallen nature from which we are not completely freed in this life. But this is not the whole truth, for the Spirit in us is life because of righteousness. The Holy Spirit is the source of true life, a foretaste and assurance of our coming resurrection life. The righteousness is Christ's righteousness, in which we are included because of our justification. And so he who raised Jesus from the dead will also give eternal life to our mortal bodies at the resurrection (verse 11). The freedom we have now in the Spirit is incomplete because we must still fight the battle against sin, and our bodies will eventually succumb to physical death. Yet the freedom we have is real because the life of the Spirit within us is the guarantee of an eternal life of perfect freedom to come.

FREEDOM AND THE LAW

Before we move on, we need to answer a question that jumps out at us from these verses: in what sense is the Old Testament law to be fulfilled in Christians? After all, we all know we are not supposed to bring bulls or lambs to church every Sunday to sacrifice! Many have been taught that we are set free from the law in such a way that it has no further role in our lives. How then can the law be so closely linked, as we have suggested, with true freedom in Christ?

It might be helpful to start by answering the question: what is the law? When we think of the "law," the first thought that comes to mind is the series of sacrificial and ceremonial requirements given to Moses for the regulation of Israel's life as a nation. These do not seem to have any relevance to us as Christians today (see further below). The law did contain many such regulations, but it also included profound moral truths concerning love of God and neighbor. Indeed, in quoting Deut. 6:5 and Lev. 19:18, Jesus defined the heart of the law as the commandments to love God with all our heart and to love our neighbor as ourselves (Mt. 22:37-40). We also usually think of the law as referring only to the Pentateuch, the first five books of the Bible. Yet twice when Jesus quoted the law, he was actually quoting the Psalms (Jn. 10:34; 15:25). The same is true of Paul. In Rom. 3:10-20, he says that "the law" pronounces judgment upon the sins of all people, and illustrates this by eight quotations from Scripture, *none of which come from the Pentateuch.* This can be easily explained. By the time of Jesus, the full Hebrew title of what we call the Old Testament became "The Law, the Prophets and the Writings," which was often shortened to "The Law." It is only by context that we know when it uses the word "law" whether the New Testament is referring to the law of Moses or to some other portion of

77

the Old Testament. The point is that the law refers to the totality of the Old Testament revelation of God.

It is true that Hebrews 7-10 understands the role of the law as both fulfilled and ended by the sacrifice of Christ on the cross. But Hebrews refers particularly to *that aspect of the law of Moses dealing with the sacrificial system*, rather than those parts dealing with timeless moral truths. These aspects of the law are indeed brought to a conclusion through the one perfect sacrifice of Christ. So it seems that there are two senses of the word, a *narrower sense* referring only to the sacrificial and ceremonial aspect of the law of Moses, which is no longer applicable to Christians, and a *wider sense* referring to the whole of the Old Testament revelation. The heart of the law is stated in God's self-revelation to Moses on Mount Sinai (Ex. 34:6). He is the gracious and compassionate God, whom the children of Israel were to become like as they followed in his ways. That is why we are to be holy as he is holy, and why we are to love as he loves. That is the true meaning of the law. It's why Jesus summed up the law as loving God and loving our neighbor.

Christian freedom, as we have suggested, can be described in two aspects: freedom from and freedom for. It is freedom *from* the power of sin and death and freedom *from* the just condemnation of the law. But it is also freedom *for* service and obedience to God. And this service to God is defined in Rom. 8:4 as fulfilling the righteous requirement of the law. How can this be? Both Paul and Jesus strongly criticize the legalism of the Jewish teachers. Paul denies we can be saved through the law. And Hebrews 7-10 teaches that the entire sacrificial system has been made obsolete through the sacrifice of Christ on the cross. To resolve this puzzle we need to understand what the purposes of the law were. Then we need to understand in what sense the law, or some aspect of it, is still valid. This is a critical question, because the understanding of our freedom in Christ is at stake.

THE PURPOSES OF THE LAW BEFORE CHRIST

According to the New Testament, the Old Testament law had a number of purposes prior to Christ. We can divide these into two groups. The first group describes the functions of the law in relation to the exposing and judging of human sin. The second group describes the functions of the law in relation to preparing us for and leading us to the Savior.

The first category could be described as a "negative" in nature, and deals with sin:

- The law defines sin as disobedience to God.
- It then sharpens that definition by transforming sin into transgression, illuminating the whole range of human conduct as willful violation of God's commands.
- It exposes the heart of legalism, in which sin masquerades as self-exalting religious ritualism.
- It pronounces the entirely righteous and just judgment of God upon all human sin, leaving no person exempt or excused.

The second category could be described as "positive" in nature, and deals with preparation:

- The law prepares us for Christ by promising and prophesying his coming.
- The law prepares us for Christ by showing his perfect obedience to its commands.
- The law prepares us for Christ by showing how his obedience contrasts with our own disobedience, showing us that our only hope of fulfilling the law is to be found in him.

•The law prepares us for Christ through its sacrificial system which provides a measure of forgiveness while pointing to full forgiveness through the sacrifice of Christ

Notice that *nowhere in this list is mentioned the possibility that God gave the law for us to be saved by it*. In fact, the opposite is the case. Paul answers this question himself: "Is the law then contrary to the promises of God? Certainly not! For if a law had been given that could give life, then righteousness would indeed be by the law. But the Scripture imprisoned everything under sin, so that the promise by faith in Jesus Christ might be given to those who believe" (Gal. 3:21-22). Paul's point is that God understood the predicament we were in due to our rebellion, yet had compassion on us. He determined to send his Son for our salvation, and guaranteed this through the promise made to Abraham that in his seed all the families of the earth would be blessed (Gen. 12:3). Abraham was apparently an idol worshipper when God called him (Josh. 24:2), and knew very little about the God who made this amazing promise to him. We would not have known much more than Abraham did about God, or what God requires of us, had God not chosen to reveal himself through Moses, the prophets and the other writers of Scripture. In the time intervening between the promise and its fulfillment, the nature and character of God had to be revealed, sin had to be defined and addressed, the covenant line had to be preserved, and humanity had to understand its need for a Savior. Hence the law and all that goes with it — the historical, prophetic and worship record of the rest of the Old Testament. All this was a gift of God and therefore of grace.

THE PURPOSES OF THE LAW IN CHRIST

The law had its purposes prior to Christ, but according to Paul the law still has an important function in the life of Christian believers. How then can we understand the relationship between Christ (or the Gospel) and the law? The clue is found in Jesus' own words: "Do not think that I have come to abolish the Law or the Prophets; I have not come to abolish them but to fulfill them. For truly I say to you, until heaven and earth pass away, not an iota, not a dot, will pass from the Law until all is accomplished. Therefore whoever relaxes one of the least of these commandments and teaches others to do the same will be called least in the kingdom of heaven, but whoever does them and teaches them will be called great in the kingdom of heaven. For I tell you, unless your righteousness exceeds that of the scribes and Pharisees, you will never enter the kingdom of heaven" (Mt. 5:17-20). The important point is this: "until all is accomplished" and "until heaven and earth pass away" are equated by Jesus, and *together identified as the conclusion of the period in which the law will be valid.* At that point, the law will no longer be necessary, for we will have entered into perfect union with Christ. To suppose that "until all is accomplished" represents the work of Christ on the cross, and that the law is thus no longer valid, is not what Jesus said at all! The kingdom of heaven is what Jesus proclaimed. It is the kingdom in which we have been living since Pentecost. Jesus repeatedly identified his ministry as bringing in the kingdom of heaven (though not yet in its final form), and states here that those who obey the law will be greatest in this kingdom, while those who break the law will be the least. Jesus' final point underlines his meaning. A far more genuine obedience of the law, drastically different in nature from the self-righteous practices of the Pharisees, is essential to participating in the kingdom of heaven. In this kingdom, there is no room for the legalistic perversion of the law, nor is there any need for the whole ceremonial-sacrificial system fulfilled on and ended by the cross. God requires a far greater level of righteousness to enter his kingdom, and that righteousness can only be acquired from Christ as a gift of his grace.

The heart of the law, as Jesus understood, was to love God and to love one's neighbor as oneself. "On these two commandments," he said, "depend all the Law and the Prophets" (Mt. 22:40). Jesus did not invent these two principles. He was quoting from the law itself (Deut. 6:5 and Lev. 19:18). Jesus was not a moral reformer or ethical philosopher. He was the Son of God, God himself, our Savior. He entered this world to manifest God's presence, to live a perfect life in obedience to the law, and to suffer and die for our sins. He did not come to bring a new or different ethical or moral teaching than was already present in the Old Testament. He simply expounded the teaching that was already there. He did so not simply by explaining its true meaning, but by revealing in his own Person its living fulfillment. *To see Jesus live is to see the law truly and perfectly fulfilled.*

This is what Paul means when he says that we can fulfill the righteous requirement of the law by walking in the Spirit. Jesus came so that for the first time we would be able to love God and others by the power of the Spirit and not by our own efforts. He came so that by the Spirit we could be salt and light in a darkened world, and so that we could glorify God in our conduct as husbands and wives, as members of the body, teachers and students, employees and employers, and as citizens of our nation. This fulfilling of the law is a work in progress for us, for we live in this period of the "in between," where we have the Spirit yet are still battling the flesh.

If we say that the law is abolished or of no further relevance, we reduce the Old Testament to a relic of history, valid then but not now. In that case, we might as well cut it out of our Bibles with our scissors. But please heed this warning. *If we do so, we gut the heart of Jesus' teaching and that of the apostles.* How can we understand what Jesus or Paul taught concerning love without seeing it in its original context as a reflection on the nature of the God of the Old Testament? For in the Old Testament God spelled out in great detail what love looks like — treating the poor with care and dignity, dealing honestly in business, not moving our neighbor's boundary stone, robbing him or sleeping with his wife? Modern liberal theology, by disowning the Old Testament, has replaced the law with a vague principle of love as the heart of Christian life and freedom. *But by doing so, it has emptied love of all Biblical meaning.* Without the Old Testament teaching on sanctity of life, it can be considered unloving to oppose abortion. Without the Old Testament teaching on property rights, it can be considered unloving to oppose one group of people seizing the possessions of others. Without the Old Testament teaching on marriage, it can be considered unloving to make divorce a last option. We can't understand who Jesus is without understanding who the Old Testament prophesies him to be. *Similarly, we can't understand what Jesus taught without placing it within the framework of the divine law he understood himself to be the fulfillment of.* The law was never meant to be the means of our salvation, but it did and does express the heart of the God who is its author. Without it, our freedom in Christ would soon degenerate into anarchy. We are certainly freed from the law's just condemnation by the work of Christ, However, that same work gives us freedom to fulfill the law's just requirement to love God and neighbor. We cannot say that the law has been abolished. But we do see that Jesus came to show the way to its true fulfillment in a manner the Jewish teachers, by their own self-righteous works, never understood and never achieved.

This is what Paul meant when he wrote these words: "What shall we say then? That Gentiles who did not pursue righteousness have attained it... but that Israel, who pursued a law that would lead to righteousness, did not succeed in reaching that law. Why? Because they did not pursue it by faith, but as if it were based on works" (Rom. 9:30-32). When the law is pursued by faith, Paul continues, it leads us directly to Christ, its "end" (Rom. 10:4). The word "end" *(telos)* means not a conclusion, but a goal that has been reached. The law, as Jesus said, is not abolished by him but is instead fulfilled in him.

FREEDOM AND THE SPIRIT OF ADOPTION (VERSES 12-16)

12 So then, brothers, we are debtors, not to the flesh, to live according to the flesh. 13 For if you live according to the flesh you will die, but if by the Spirit you put to death the deeds of the body, you will live. 14 For all who are led by the Spirit of God are sons of God. 15 For you did not receive the spirit of slavery to fall back into fear, but you have received the Spirit of adoption as sons, by whom we cry, "Abba! Father!" 16 The Spirit himself bears witness with our spirit that we are children of God"

With the words "So then, brothers" in verse 12, Paul draws a practical conclusion from his teaching on freedom in the Spirit in the first eleven verses of the chapter. His conclusion is that we are "debtors." We have a debt or obligation to Christ, because of what he has done for us. This obligation is to live by the Spirit, not the flesh. And if we live by the Spirit, we "will live" (verse 13b), by which he means live eternally. The putting to death of the deeds of the body is in the Greek present tense, signifying a continuous, repeated action which must be carried out as long as we live on this earth. The "deeds of the body" include everything that arises out of our fallen human nature, not just sexual immorality but also jealousy, anger, strife and dissension (Gal. 5:19-21). Why we are able to put these wicked deeds to death is explained in verse 14: "For all who are led by the Spirit of God are sons of God." We are able to put to death the deeds of the body *because* we are led by the Spirit of God, and *therefore* are sons and daughters of God. The fact that we are led by the Spirit reveals that we are God's sons and daughters. Our freedom as believers is the fruit of a life we have been given through the Spirit as the sons and daughters of God.

The Holy Spirit we have received is not a spirit of slavery leading us back into fear, but is the Spirit of adoption (verse 15a). Paul could have said that the opposite to the spirit of slavery is the Spirit of freedom, but he used the word "adoption" instead. This shows that he equates freedom with adoption. *It is the sons and daughters who are free.* The more deeply we realize what it is to be a son or daughter of God, the more freedom we will enter into. This is not a freedom of independence (as the world defines freedom) but of utter dependency. The Bible, as it so often does, turns the thinking of the world on its head. It is by the Spirit that we cry out, "Abba, Father" (verse 15b). Paul was certainly thinking of how Jesus taught his disciples to address God as "Father." The word "Abba" represents an Aramaic word for "father." Originally used by small children as the equivalent of "daddy," it had by the time of Jesus come into more general use as a word for "father." A grown man, for instance, might address his father as *abba.* So the popular translation of this phrase in more than a few sermons as "daddy" is probably not accurate. Nevertheless, it's important to point out that the word was never used in Judaism as a form of address to God. *No one, in fact, before Jesus had ever addressed God as "Father" using this form of intimate terminology.* The revolutionary significance of this fact is often overlooked. When Jesus addressed God in this way, he was drawing attention to the intimacy of relationship the word expressed. We have now been adopted into this relationship through Christ, and this is made real in our lives through the work of the Holy Spirit. Paul expresses the same idea elsewhere: "And because you are sons, God has sent the Spirit of his Son into our hearts, crying, 'Abba! Father!' So you are no longer a slave, but a son, and if a son, then an heir through God" (Gal. 3:6-7).

The Holy Spirit "bears witness with" (assures) our spirit that we are the children of God (verse 16). To recognize God as our Father, and ourselves as his children, is at the very heart of Christian faith, which is about relationship, not religion. *To recognize God as Father represents freedom.* But it also represents the fulfilling of the law spoken of in verse 4. Why is this so? Because as we cry out to God as Father and recognize him as such, we are placing ourselves under his authority and asking for his character to be reproduced in us. As children, we want to be like the Father. As Cranfield puts it: "For to address the true God by the name of Father with full sincerity and seriousness will involve seeking wholeheartedly to be and think and say and do that which is pleasing to him." This is freedom, and this is the fulfilling of the law in us who walk according to the Spirit.

THE SPIRIT GIVES FREEDOM IN THE MIDST OF SUFFERING (VERSES 17-30)

17 and if children, then heirs—heirs of God and fellow heirs with Christ, provided we suffer with him in order that we may also be glorified with him.

18 For I consider that the sufferings of this present time are not worth comparing with the glory that is to be revealed to us. 19 For the creation waits with eager longing for the revealing of the sons of God. 20 For the creation was subjected to futility, not willingly, but because of him who subjected it, in hope 21 that the creation itself will be set free from its bondage to corruption and obtain the freedom of the glory of the children of God.

As a result of the work of Christ, the Holy Spirit has brought us into a new life of freedom, freedom from the law's just condemnation and slavery to sin, and freedom for obedience to God. Yet this life of freedom must be lived out in a world that is anything but free. And we ourselves still live in this fallen world, and are affected by the fallout of our ancestor's sin. We live in the "in-between," that place where Christ has set us free, and yet the final fulfillment of that freedom remains to be achieved. The freedom the Holy Spirit has given us does not result in an instant translation to a trouble-free life. The freedom of the Spirit is something experienced in our inner being, and gives us strength to endure when our external freedom is limited by adversity and suffering. In a fallen world, we will encounter suffering. Suffering is a limitation to freedom.

Suffering comes as a result of the general fallenness of the world — we all become sick and we all die. But the suffering Paul is especially thinking of here is that which comes as a direct result of our following Jesus. We walk in the way of the cross. Because of the true inner freedom we can never lose, we are willing to give up some external freedoms if it expresses obedience to God or leads to the advancement of the gospel. And so Paul says we are heirs "provided we suffer with him in order that we may also be glorified with him" (verse 17). The fact of our present suffering, far from calling into question our future inheritance, is actually an assurance of our coming glorification.

Yet, he continues, the sufferings of this present time are by no means comparable to this coming glory (verse 18). The meaning of this statement is clarified in verses 19-30. These verses explain the tension between present suffering and future glory, the present limitation of our freedom and its future fulfillment. They speak of the reality of hope for the believer in the midst of the difficult challenges of life.

Before he turns to this topic, he points out that the physical creation itself longs for the freedom that will come with the "revealing of the sons of God" (verse 19). In this present age, it has been subjected to "futility" or frustration (verse 20). This word refers to something which fails to reach its goal. The creation has been unable to fulfill the purpose of its existence, which is to reflect the glory of the One who created it. Paul is thinking here of the curse God placed on the earth in Gen. 3:17: "Cursed is the ground because of you." Creation cannot fulfill its purpose so long as humanity is not fully restored to God. Ecological movements without a Christian basis and empty of the power of the Holy Spirit will be limited by the fact they have no ability to change the hearts of the people who treat the environment badly. The one subjecting the creation to futility must be God (rather than Satan) because only he could have subjected it "in hope." As a result of the curse, God has limited even the freedom of the physical creation to express what it was created for. The content of the hope is that the "creation itself will be set free from its bondage to corruption and obtain the freedom of the glory of the children of God" (verse 21). Paul does not mean, of course, that the creation will enjoy the same freedom as the children of God, but that when the children of God come into their freedom, the creation will attain its own proper freedom to reflect perfectly the glory of its Creator. The thought that the creation, even though it may be radically transformed into a "new heaven and a new earth," will be renewed rather than simply discarded, should make us, as Christians, the very best stewards of the creation as it exists now, even as we are also to steward our own physical bodies on account of our belief in their resurrection.

22 For we know that the whole creation has been groaning together in the pains of childbirth until now. 23 And not only the creation, but we ourselves, who have the firstfruits of the Spirit, groan inwardly as we wait eagerly for adoption as sons, the redemption of our bodies. 24 For in this hope we were saved. Now hope that is seen is not hope. For who hopes for what he sees? 25 But if we hope for what we do not see, we wait for it with patience.

We, like the creation, groan as if in childbirth. Paul borrows the Old Testament idea of Zion groaning to bring forth her children (Isa. 26:17;

66:8; Jer. 4:31), and applies it both to Christians and to the created world, though obviously each groans in a different manner. The firstfruits in the Old Testament were a gift of humanity to God of the initial part of the harvest signifying the full tithe yet to come. Here, Paul reverses the idea. God is now giving the firstfruits to humanity. The firstfruits is the present working of the Holy Spirit in our hearts. This is a gift guaranteeing the fullness of his work in us in eternity. It is not the Spirit himself who is the first fruits, but rather *his present work in us.* If the Spirit were the firstfruits, it would diminish who he is, by suggesting that in the future life we would have something more or better than him.

We groan, awaiting our adoption, the redemption of our bodies (verse 23). In verses 14-16, Paul stated that we are already the children of God, having received the Spirit of adoption. Yet here he suggests our adoption is still to come. The key to understanding this tension is provided by the phrase in verse 19 concerning the "revealing of the sons of God." We are sons and daughters, yet our sonship has *yet to be revealed* to all creation. In the same way, we *are adopted*, yet the *public manifestation of that adoption* will only occur at the return of the Lord, at the redemption of our bodies, our final deliverance from mortality. In this present life, we live under the effects of sin. We are free in Christ, yet this freedom does not extend to our mortal bodies. We are free from eternal death, but not physical death. We are free from the stranglehold of sin, but must still fight against it. In short, we were saved in hope (verse 24). Our freedom is real because of the work of the Spirit within us, yet it is not complete. We hope in patience for what we do not yet see (verse 25). That patience itself is a fruit of the Spirit's work in us (Gal. 5:22). In 5:5, Paul reminds us that this hope does not disappoint us, because God's love floods our hearts by his Spirit. The freedom the Spirit has given us is the assurance its fulfillment will certainly come.

26 Likewise the Spirit helps us in our weakness. For we do not know what to pray for as we ought, but the Spirit himself intercedes for us with groanings too deep for words. 27 And he who searches hearts knows what is the mind of the Spirit, because the Spirit intercedes for the saints according to the will of God.

This work of the Spirit is powerful. The word "likewise" in verse 26 links the way in which we as believers groan (verse 23) and the way in which the Spirit himself groans, interceding for us with "groanings too deep for words." God himself comes down to us in the Person of his Spirit and travails in this birth process even within our weak and sinful hearts as we cry out to him. This is one of the most powerful pictures of the grace of God in the entire Bible. These groanings of the Spirit are effective, for God himself, who searches our hearts, knows the mind of the Spirit (verse 27). The Old Testament often pictures God as the searcher of our hearts (1 Sam. 16:7; Ps. 7:9; 44:21). If he knows the secrets of our hearts, he must certainly know the desires of his own Spirit, who is interceding for the saints according to his will. These groanings of the Spirit bring freedom to our troubled hearts in the midst of external challenges and restrictions.

28 And we know that for those who love God all things work together for good, for those who are called according to his purpose.

This verse is known and loved by all believers, but the significance of its structure is often overlooked. The phrase "for those who love God" is placed in Greek at the beginning of the sentence, rather than later on as would normally be the case. This has the effect of making these words emphatic. It is *for those who love God and those people only* that the following promise applies, but to them it does apply and can be counted on. For such people "all things work together for good." But what are the "all things"? The "all things" that he refers to are the "sufferings of the present time" referred to in verse 18, and further alluded to in the next section. *This verse is not an assurance that believers will be spared from trouble, but that in the trouble they will undoubtedly face they can know that God is with them.* Our freedom, in other words, is not dependent on external circumstances, but on the work of the Holy Spirit in our hearts. The freedom we have on the inside compensates for whatever lack we suffer on the outside due to living in this fallen world. And some of what we suffer comes as a result of our testimony to Christ. The New Testament assumes that there is a cost to discipleship. It is through many tribulations that we enter the kingdom of God (Ac. 14:22). A gospel that promises an easy life is a false gospel. What we need to know is that when the tough times come, the grace of God is powerful enough to carry us through them. We have freedom to serve God in the laying down of our lives, but God will keep us in the midst of it with a freedom no one can take away from us, which is rooted in the presence of his Spirit and the hope of future deliverance.

The phrase "for good" is of great importance, for it is God alone who can truly define the "good." The "good" represents his will for us. It may not represent our comfort or pleasure in the short term, but it is what will ultimately give us joy as God works out his plan in our lives. *Believers must choose to allow God to define the "good."* If we try to define it to suit our own desires, we will quickly find out that God is not responding to our prayers by producing the results that we want. But for the obedient believer, even the difficult things (such as the tribulations of verse 35) are part of the "good" that God is working out in our lives. The fact that we are "called according to his purpose" brings out the fact that God has a destiny for each one of us, and true freedom in this life will only come in pursuing it. The mention of our being called underlines the fact that our very ability to love God and live for him comes out of his prior calling of us. Or, as John expressed it, "We love because he first loved us" (1 Jn. 4:19).

29 For those whom he foreknew he also predestined to be conformed to the image of his Son, in order that he might be the firstborn among many brothers. 30 And those whom he predestined he also called, and those whom he called he also justified, and those whom he justified he also glorified.

In this present life, we may feel anything but free as we battle the desires of the flesh, live in the midst of a rebellious world and are reminded daily of our mortality. But in these two verses, Paul steps back to view our situation from the perspective of eternity. This perspective gives us confidence in the utter sovereignty of the God who gives true freedom even in the midst of the adversities life throws at us. In verses 29-30, he employs a chain of five verbs to describe God's gracious choosing of his people. *First,* God foreknew us. Included in the Hebrew concept of God's knowing a person is God's knowing his purpose for the person. This "knowing" occurs before creation, in the realm of God's eternal existence. *Second,* God "predestined us to be conformed to the image of his Son." This verb describes God's gracious decision, taken before the world's foundation, concerning the purpose for which he created us — we are to become like Christ. The "being conformed" speaks of the process of sanctification in this life, not just our future glory. *God cannot foreknow a person and the purpose for which they were created without also having a plan to implement what is contained in his knowledge.* Paul is undoubtedly thinking of the restoration of the image of God in which Adam was created (Gen. 1:27). Before humanity fell, God had put in place his plan of redemption. Before a disaster happens to you, God has a plan to bring good out of it. *Third,* "Those whom he predestined he also called." The verb "called" brings us out of eternity and into the history of our encounter with Christ. God's calling and our conversion are two sides of the same coin. Though God holds us accountable for our responses, the Bible always places the emphasis on the sovereign action of God. We do have free will, but from whom do we receive that free will? It is far better to err on the side of curtailing the free will of humanity than to err on the side of curtailing the sovereignty of God, for without an utterly sovereign God we as his creatures are nothing. A limited God is no God at all. But a sovereign God gives freedom. *Fourth*, God has "justified" those he called. *Fifth*, "those whom he justified he also glorified." Being justified we can understand, but how can Paul say we have already been glorified? From God's perspective, our glorification has already been assured. Even though it still has to be worked out in our lives, its fulfillment is so certain it can be spoken of as an accomplished fact.

THE TRIUMPH OF GOD'S LOVE (VERSES 31-39)

31 What then shall we say to these things? If God is for us, who can be against us? 32 He who did not spare his own Son but gave him up for us all, how will he not also with him graciously give us all things? 33 Who shall bring any charge against God's elect? It is God who justifies. 34 Who is to condemn? Christ Jesus is the one who died — more than that, who was raised — who is at the right hand of God, who indeed is interceding for us. 35 Who shall separate us from the love of Christ? Shall tribulation, or distress, or persecution, or famine, or nakedness, or danger, or sword? 36 As it is written, "For your sake we are being killed all the day long; we are regarded as sheep to be slaughtered." 37 No, in all these things we are more than conquerors through him who loved us. 38 For I am sure that neither death nor life, nor angels nor rulers, nor things present nor things to come, nor powers, 39 nor height nor depth, nor anything else in all creation, will be able to separate us from the love of God in Christ Jesus our Lord.

"What then shall we say to these things?" Paul asks in verse 31. His next words, "If God is for us," are a good summary of the entire letter to the Romans. His rhetorical question "Who can be against us?" is a declaration that nothing anyone could do to us can threaten our freedom in Christ or our eternal inheritance. If God did not spare his own Son, Paul continues in verse 32, how will he not with Christ give us all things? He "gave him up for us all." Here Paul uses the same verb as in 1:24, 26, 28, where God gave humanity over to the consequences of their sin. What amazing grace, that he who justly gave us over on account of our sin, should give his Son over to rescue us from his judgment on those very transgressions! No one can bring any charge against those God has justified (verse 33). God has declared the verdict of "not guilty," and no one can reverse the verdict that set us free.

Next come three statements about Christ, in ascending order of significance: Christ died, was raised from the dead and is now at the right hand of God (verse 34). He intercedes for us, with all the approval and power of heaven behind him. What, then, shall separate us from the love of Christ (verse 35)? Paul offers a list of seven forms of trial, all of which involve loss of outward freedom, only to respond that none of these can separate us from Christ or take from us the true inner freedom he has given us. He was not speaking theoretically, for he himself had experienced six of the seven tribulations — and by the time his life ended (if ancient tradition is correct), would experience the sword also. Christians may lose outward freedom for the sake of the gospel, but their suffering only makes more certain possession of the perfect freedom that is coming.

As verse 37 states: "In all these things we are more than conquerors through him who loved us." Our freedom to live as servants of Christ cannot be stolen from us by persecution or any other adversity. God meets us in the troubles, and it is precisely there that we find the victory. The Gospel does not promise an easy life. Paul uses the word "tribulation" *(thlipsis)* 33 times, and at least 31 of those are clear references to our present Christian life. The same is true in Revelation, which reminds us the tribulation is a present reality, not one referring to a very limited period just before Christ's return. To follow Jesus is to embrace adversity. Suffering is not an end in itself, but God works the tough times together for good in his eternal plan. Too often, the church in our pleasure-oriented culture has foolishly tried to make the Gospel attractive by portraying it as a cure for all our problems, and then we wonder why people become disillusioned when God does not make good on the "promises" he has supposedly made.

38 For I am sure that neither death nor life, nor angels nor rulers, nor things present nor things to come, nor powers, 39 nor height nor depth, nor anything else in all creation, will be able to separate us from the love of God in Christ Jesus our Lord.

The truth is that nothing in heaven or on earth can separate us from God's love in Christ (verse 38). Paul sets forth in verses 38-39 a list of all the possible things which might cause a separation and take away our inner freedom. "Death" cannot do it, for Christ has triumphed over death and opened the gates of eternal life. "Life" cannot do it — that is, "life" understood as standing for all the troubles, disappointments and challenges life brings, for God works these together for good. Neither can "angels" or "rulers" — by which Paul means those heavenly forces over which Christ has triumphed in the cross (Col. 2:15). Neither can "things present" or "things to come," for all of history is under Christ's control. Nor can "powers" — probably a further reference to supernatural beings. Neither can "height" or "depth." Perhaps he is thinking here of Ps. 139:8: "If I ascend to heaven, you are there! If I make my bed in Sheol, you are there!" The list concludes with "nor anything else in all creation." His intention is to declare as emphatically as possible that absolutely nothing in all creation can separate us from "the love of God in Christ Jesus our Lord" (verse 39). The name and title of Christ, used in 5:1 to begin Paul's exposition of the Christian life, is used to conclude each one of its chapters (5:21, 6:23, 7:25 and 8:39). Christ is indeed all and in

SIX

FREEDOM AND
THE FULFILLING OF THE LAW

8 Owe no one anything, except to love each other, for the one who loves another has fulfilled the law. 9 For the commandments, 'You shall not commit adultery, You shall not commit murder, You shall not steal, You shall not covet,' and any other commandment, are summed up in this one word: 'You shall love your neighbor as yourself.' 10 Love does no wrong to a neighbor; therefore, love is the fulfilling of the law. (Rom. 13:8-10)

What is so important about this short passage is the fact that in it Paul sums up all his ethical teaching in the one overarching commandment of love. This shows us that the goal of freedom is to love both God and others. What is so interesting about this statement is how closely related it is to the fulfilling of the law. The exercise of our freedom is closely related to how the law is fulfilled in our lives. Why this is so becomes evident as the passage unfolds.

In the previous verses (Rom. 13:1-7), dealing with the Christian's obligation to the state, Paul has made it clear we are to pay our debts. He repeats this here, yet adds the phrase "except to love one another." The debt of love will always remain outstanding. We can never perfectly pay it. Why this is so is explained in the next phrase: "for the one who loves another has fulfilled the law." We may be able to fulfill the requirements of civil law by paying our taxes, but we can never completely fulfill the requirements of God's law. If we did, we would be perfect men and women, not imperfect believers who have sinned and yet still fall short of God's standard (Rom. 3:23).

As in Rom. 8:4, it is the law which is to be fulfilled. With rare exceptions where the "law of sin" is referred to (Rom. 7:24; 8:2), Paul almost invariably uses the word "law" in reference to the Old Testament law. That, for him, represented what his entire Hebrew Bible was called ("The Law, the Prophets and the Writings," or "The Law" for short). That's why, even when he quotes the Psalms, he refers to it as "the law" (see Rom. 3:19, where quotations in the preceding verses from the Psalms, Proverbs, Isaiah and Jeremiah are all referred to as coming from "the law"). The heart of the Old Testament was the law given to Moses, but for Paul and other Jews the law referred to the whole Bible as they had it. So when the law is to be fulfilled, the reference is to the teachings of the whole Old Testament, not just the Mosaic law.

But here in verse 9 Paul is quoting directly from the words of Moses (Exod. 20:13-17: Deut. 5:17-21). He cites four of the commandments, then adds the phrase "and any other commandment," just to make sure no one thought it was only these four which remained valid for Christian believers. He then sums up the whole law, as did Jesus, with the phrase

"You shall love your neighbor as yourself" (Lev. 19:18).

It is an enormous misunderstanding to think that Paul rejected the Old Testament law, and thought of the freedom in the Spirit he has described in 8:2 (as well as Gal. 5:1) as consisting in a vague and undefined command to love instead. The command to love is valid simply because it is part of the Old Testament law. This raises the question of what Jesus meant when he said: "A new commandment I give to you, that you love one another: just as I have loved you, you also are to love one another" (Jn. 13:34). Is Jesus substituting love for the law? After all, we were in slavery under the law, but now we are free in Christ. Perhaps this freedom is defined simply as love, or at least to love as Christ did?

That would be a hasty conclusion. Jesus taught that love for God and neighbor was the heart of the Mosaic law — you shall love the Lord your God and you shall love your neighbor as yourself (Mk. 12:28-33). His command to love is not "new" because it's different from what went before. It's new because Jesus himself for the first time revealed the full meaning of what love for God and neighbor is (Jn. 8:29; 10:18; 12:49-50; 14:51; 15:10). And it is new in the sense that it will become the hallmark of the new messianic community created by the coming of the Holy Spirit at Pentecost.

And the Jewish teachers knew this. After all, the Pharisee who asked Jesus what the most important commandment in the law was wholeheartedly agreed with his answer (Mk. 12:32). There is a whole list of Rabbis who found love to be the unifying principle of the law. Not one of them would have thought that love is something separate from the other commandments. They knew that all the commandments, in one way or another, show us how to love. Paul says here that the law is "summed up" in the command to love. What he means is not that love is an undefined principle somehow different from or greater than the law. It is that love is involved in every single commandment of the law, even those involving sacrificial and ceremonial aspects. That includes everything from the general command to love God to the command not to move our neighbor's boundary stone. The difference between Paul and the Rabbis is that Paul understood the ceremonial aspects to be fulfilled in the sacrifice of Christ on the cross, such that we are no longer subject to them (and also that he understood the full meaning of love in the light of the cross). But that is by no means all the Old Testament amounted to.

And so the fulfillment of the law is love. What Paul says here is the same as he said in Rom. 8:4: the believer is set free in Christ (8:2) in order to be able to begin a genuine, grace-empowered fulfillment of the law. This fulfillment is real freedom, because it is not achieved through human effort in order to promote our own standing with God, as if we could obligate God to accept us on the basis of good works we have done. The fulfillment comes instead through the Spirit by believers already accepted by God, who then allow the love of God to become ever increasingly the motivation for all their actions. A vague and general command to love is both meaningless and dangerous. It allows us, not God, to judge what love looks like. It causes love to degenerate into undefined, sentimental and hypocritical generalities. It is the love of Hollywood or pagan culture, or even the love of a sentimental greeting card. It is dangerous because it causes people who practice this kind of love to live in a deception that they are good people and will find their own way to heaven, even while they walk through life in a self-centered, self-righteous, self-deluded haze.

The fact that the debt to love remains outstanding as long as we live highlights our own fallenness and inadequacy. The fact we are redeemed does not mean we are fully free from the effects of sin and the curse. We need the external standard provided by the Scriptures as a guide, and also as a continual reminder we still have a distance to travel.

We have been *freed from* sin and the just condemnation of the law, but the other side of the coin is we have been *freed for* love, whether love of God or love of others. When we reach the new Jerusalem, our freedom will still have as its goal love and obedience to God. But there, we will no longer need the external guide of the Scriptures, for we will live in perfect fellowship with God. Our obedience will be expressed fully and naturally in our relationship with the Father. But for now, we need that daily reminder that our freedom must be exercised within certain boundaries. God's law provides the continual and greatly needed guide directing our attention away from ourselves, and toward him and others. Freedom for the Christian can never be a goal in itself. That would be nothing more than the ultimate expression of self-centeredness. Freedom without external boundaries will inevitably be corrupted into a form of self-fulfillment and turn into slavery to the world, the flesh and the devil.

Neither freedom nor love can be exalted as a principle divorced from the concrete commands of Scripture. The vacuum left when Scripture is removed as the unbreakable standard is quickly filled by the personal preferences of those who follow that way. The content rarely comes from God. God went to great pains to give clear and explicit definition to what love is. Our sin in the Garden was to taste of the fruit of the tree of the knowledge of good and evil. Ever since that day, fallen human nature has sought to determine good and evil, right and wrong, always with a view to what benefits us personally. God gave his law to draw us out of that spiritual and moral morass. Now at last, because of the work of Christ and the gift of the Spirit, we can see a genuine beginning of the law's fulfillment in our lives.

13For you were called to freedom, brothers. Only do not use your freedom as an opportunity for the flesh, but through love serve one another. 14For the whole law is fulfilled in one word: 'You shall love your neighbor as yourself.' 15 But if you bite and devour one another, watch out that you are not consumed by one another. (Gal. 5:13-15)

Paul has spent most of Galatians up to this point warning against those who misuse the law as a means to self-justification. But in 5:13, he abruptly switches direction. He wants to make sure no one mistakes him as saying you can throw the Scriptures overboard and live without them. Freedom is not the ability to do whatever we want, but it paradoxically comes to us in the form of a different kind of slavery: we are to serve (literally be slaves) of one another. The possession of the freedom Christ has won for us at such great cost must not be allowed to degenerate into pursuit of our own selfish desires. And so arises the great paradox of Christian freedom: *freedom can only be preserved through service to God and others.* The exercise of freedom is the same as the exercise of love.

And love must be understood within the framework of God's law. By living in freedom through loving our neighbor as ourselves, we fulfill "the whole law" (verse 14). There is an unusual placing of the adjective "all" here, which has the force of emphasizing that *every single aspect* of the law is involved. The law is truly obeyed when each of its commands is fulfilled in love. The law possesses an inner unity in which all of its commands express the same characteristic of love. The gospel frees us from the need to win God's approval through our own performance of the law, which in our fallen nature we cannot do. But by giving us God's acceptance as a free gift in Christ, the gospel frees us for the first time to obey the law in a genuine, if not perfect way. When we fulfill the commands in the love that God has given us in Christ, they are truly fulfilled.

16 But I say, walk by the Spirit, and you will not gratify the desires of the flesh. 17 For the desires of the flesh are against the Spirit, and the desires of the Spirit are against the flesh, for these are opposed to each other, to keep you from doing the things you want to do. 18 But if you are led by the Spirit, you are not under the law.

Paul reinforces this in the next verses. He states here what he has been insisting on since the beginning of the letter. The work of Christ on the cross has delivered us from the just condemnation of the law (verse 18). This is made effective in us through the power of the Spirit (verse 16). The flesh cannot be overcome by our own unaided attempts at obedience to the law, but only by the work of the Spirit (verse 17). He goes on to give a lengthy list of both vices and virtues in verses 19-23, which serves further to remind us that a general principle of love divorced from the commands of Scripture will do nothing to address the battle against the flesh. The vices and virtues in the list are all things that are respectively condemned and commanded in the Old Testament law. Paul adds nothing new. To be truly free in Christ means to live in the power of the Spirit to see the character of Christ daily formed in us according to God's law.

2 Bear one another's burdens, and so fulfill the law of Christ. (Gal. 6:2)

Next we turn to Galatians 6, and there we find the same idea. To bear one another's burdens is surely the same thing as loving one's neighbor as oneself. In both Romans and Galatians, Paul connects that love with the freedom we are given to fulfill the law by the power of the Spirit. So does the "law of Christ" then refer to the Old Testament law as fulfilled in Christ? Yes it does, for when Paul uses the word "law," he almost always refers to the Old Testament law (or the Old Testament as a whole). To suggest that the "law of Christ" is a vague and undefined kind of law or principle consisting of love, but disconnected from the Old Testament, is a thought completely without foundation elsewhere in Paul's writings.

Let's briefly trace Paul's line of thinking in Galatians. Christ has redeemed us from the curse of the law (the law's just punishment on our sin) by fulfilling the law perfectly and carrying our sins on the cross (Gal. 3:12-13). He never intended that we be saved by our own efforts at law fulfillment, and so the law is not contrary to the promises of God (Gal. 3:21). The law pronounced God's judgment on sin (Gal. 3:22a), so that the promise would come by faith through the work of Christ (Gal. 3:22b). The law was our guardian to lead us to Christ (Gal. 3:24-25). We are now, in Christ, sons and daughters of God according to the promise given to Abraham (Gal. 3:26-29).

When Paul looks at the Jewish legalists, the religious establishment which crucified Jesus, he sees people who twisted and perverted God's intention for the law, which was actually to lead us to Christ. They attempted to make it into an instrument for their own self-righteousness and the propagation of their false religious system. This is what Paul declares to be the present Jerusalem which is in slavery (Gal. 4:24). He is not speaking of Joshua, David and the great prophets who exhorted Israel to obey the law. There is nothing wrong with the law. In fact, the law is holy and righteous and good (Rom. 7:12).

The new covenant, however, is a covenant of freedom: "For freedom Christ has set us free" (Gal. 5:1). As Hebrews 7-10 explains in detail, Christ has fulfilled the sacrificial and ceremonial aspects of the law. As a result, we no longer need to be circumcised, sacrifice bulls on the altar, cut our hair in Nazirite vows, or wear garments made of only one fabric. So when the Jewish legalists infiltrated the Galatian church and informed them they need to be circumcised to be saved, Paul puts his foot down. And that is why we get this very strong critique of Jewish legalism in the letter.

Yet after he has finished saying all this, he comes to the statement in 5:13-14 that Christian freedom involves a different kind of fulfillment of the law than the Jewish legalists were proposing. This true fulfillment of the law is for Paul summed up in the command of Lev. 19:18: "You shall love your neighbor as yourself." Believers take hold of this fulfillment by being "led by the Spirit" (Gal. 5:18). Walking in freedom in the Spirit is described in 6:2 as fulfilling the "law of Christ." *The New Testament adds no unique moral content to the law. It illustrates in the person of Christ what perfect obedience to the law looks like.* It shows us how to walk in the freedom of obedience by the Spirit. And it offers an extended description of what true fulfillment of the law by those in Christ is meant to look like. An example of this occurs in the listing of the fruit of the Spirit in Gal. 5:22-23. All of these characteristics are drawn from the instruction of the Old Testament, but are now placed into operation in believers' lives through the empowering of the Spirit.

This is reinforced when we look at how Jesus regarded the law, for Jesus' teaching on the law was the well from which Paul drew. Where Jesus uses the word "law," it refers to the Old Testament, either with reference to the first five books, or in its wider meaning of "The Law, the Prophets and the Writings." This is no vague principle of undefined love. That is clear from the way he teases out the true and deep requirements of the law in the Sermon on the Mount. At the center of that teaching is Jesus' statement that he has not come to abolish the law but to fulfill it (Mt. 5:17). He then gives some examples. The law forbids murder, but now in Christ we understand that murder begins with anger. The law forbids adultery, but now in Christ we learn that adultery begins with the eyes. The law forbids divorce, but in Christ we learn that the way the Jewish teachers had diluted the law's teaching is unacceptable, and that marriage is instituted by God. The law teaches we must honor commitments we have made (oaths), but the Jewish teachers let people off the hook through technicalities. The law teaches a principle of retribution (eye for an eye), which is meant to limit revenge, but the Jewish teachers took it as a license for revenge. By contrast, Jesus teaches on forgiveness. Judgment will be exacted (as Revelation shows in its repeated use of the "eye for an eye" principle), but it will be exacted by God. As the Sermon on the Mount continues, Jesus fleshes out the Old Testament command to love others by extending the boundaries of our love to include all people, not just those who love us in return. He denounces superficial adherence to the law's teaching on giving, prayer and fasting. He brings out the true meaning of the law's warnings against pursuit of worldly wealth. The Sermon on the Mount shows us that Jesus' goal was to bring us into a new and much deeper relationship with the heart of God as expressed through his law.

And that is what Paul describes as the law of Christ. He is applying the teaching of Jesus in the Sermon on the Mount. To bear one another's burdens, therefore, is to fulfill the law of Christ. The bearing of one another's burdens is the loving of our neighbor as ourselves. It is the fulfilling of all the commands God set down in his law, as illuminated by the perfect obedience of Christ and the teaching of the apostles. It is no new law. It is the old law, renewed in Christ, minus the sacrificial/ceremonial system. What has changed is us. We are now able, by the power of the Spirit, to begin to fulfill this law in a genuine if imperfect manner, and so bring glory to God. And that is the ultimate goal of Christian freedom.

SEVEN

FREEDOM AND
THE STATE

1 Let every person be subject to the governing authorities. For there is no authority except from God, and those that exist have been instituted by God. 2 Therefore whoever resists the authorities resists what God has appointed, and those who resist will incur judgment. 3 For rulers are not a terror to good conduct, but to bad. Would you have no fear of the one who is in authority? Then do what is good, and you will receive his approval, 4 for he is God's servant for your good. But if you do wrong, be afraid, for he does not bear the sword in vain. For he is the servant of God, an avenger who carries out God's wrath on the wrongdoer. 5 Therefore one must be in subjection, not only to avoid God's wrath but also for the sake of conscience. 6 For because of this you also pay taxes, for the authorities are ministers of God, attending to this very thing. 7 Pay to all what is owed to them: taxes to whom taxes are owed, revenue to whom revenue is owed, respect to whom respect is owed, honor to whom honor is owed. (Rom. 13:1-7)

To understand this passage properly, it must be read together with verses

8-10, examined in the previous chapter, which deal with the ongoing debt of love that all believers owe. The theme of a debt owed in verse 7 reappears in verse 8. The difference is that the debt of verse 7 consists of taxes which must be paid, and the debt of verse 8 is that of love, which can never fully be paid, and therefore always remains outstanding. Part of the debt of love owed to our neighbors involves *our relationship with them in the context of civil society.* And that is the subject of verses 1-7.

Being a citizen involves giving up of some of our external freedoms. That is made clear in the first statement: "Let every person be subject to the governing authorities." Paul's choice of words is very significant. He uses the word *hupotassesthai,* "subject yourself," rather than any of the available Greek words for "obey" (*peitharkein, peithesthai* or *hupakouein*). To subject myself to someone does not indicate simple obedience, but rather the recognition that the other person has a claim on me greater in some sense than the claim I have on myself. It is used, for instance, of the wife submitting to her husband, whereas by contrast Paul uses the verb "obey" to express the action of children toward parents. The verb *hupotassesthai* means literally to place oneself under an "order," in this case, the order (Greek *taxis*) by which God has structured all human society. *When we submit, we come under an order that God has instituted for the benefit of everyone.* The existence of the order implies that each person must give up some measure of the exercise of their external freedom, for if everyone were free to do what they wanted, the result would be the strong exerting their rights at the expense of the weak. In the marriage *taxis,* the wife gives up the power of independent decision making, but the husband is commanded to love his wife and lay his life down for her as Christ did for us. So each person sacrifices some of their freedom for the greater good (see chapter eleven for a discussion of freedom in marriage). And civil society works the same way on a broader scale.

Believers cannot live in isolation from society, because by doing so they take away from the world its character as God's creation. God created the world to function harmoniously and with an order that benefits all. Our sin and rebellion has disrupted that order, but it still exists, albeit in imperfect form. But even imperfect order is far better than no order, for Satan is the author of anarchy and confusion. Christian servanthood, therefore, does not take place only in the family or in church. It takes place in civil society as well. The reason for this is not because civil society or government has any authority on its own merits, but because God himself has granted it authority to act on behalf of the betterment of all citizens. All citizens, including Christians, encounter authority primarily in the restrictions authority places on their own spontaneous desires. Submission to laws and rules that limit freedom are not just an evil to be endured, but are a good to be embraced as an expression of love for neighbor and obedience to God. And that, sadly for many of us, involves paying taxes!

That this goes against the grain for most of us is obvious. This is especially true in western societies, where we have made an idol of what we define as freedom, and in so doing have often confused political and Biblical concepts of freedom. And so it is important that we understand why political freedom is not the ultimate good or goal which will resolve all problems in human relationships. Freedom, contrary to the anti-Christian author Ayn Rand (perplexingly admired by some believers), is not an end in itself. Like everything else in our lives as believers, the exercise of freedom in a civil context must be subject to the requirements of God. The reason for this restriction is provided in these verses. The state is an authority ordained by God to provide an order in society for the benefit of all citizens, and to organize individual efforts and abilities toward the end of attaining this goal. This means that Christian believers, through subjection to the authorities, find another means to contribute to the welfare of those around them.

In a perfect world, each citizen could be entrusted with absolute freedom to do what they wanted, and such will indeed be the case in the eternal kingdom. But we live in a fallen world which is far from perfect, where even believers still struggle in the battle against their own sin. God has established the state to protect all citizens, especially those most vulnerable, against the consequences of human sin. A society of maximum personal freedom would quickly degenerate into the rule of the powerful at the expense of the weak. Paul rejects the idea of the absolute freedom of the Christian in relation to the state for the same reason he rejects absolute freedom in any other area of the believer's life — because of our weakness and imperfection.

It is important to remember what Paul is saying here. In spite of the fact that the governing authorities may be entirely unaware of the fact their authority is only delegated to them by God, they are nevertheless being used by God to attain the common good. God himself provided an example of a compassionate and just form of government under the old covenant, which itself required a measure of submission of all citizens, including the king himself. Now Paul informs us that God has established all governments, even those which fail to acknowledge him. The government Paul was calling the Roman Christians to honor was led by a bloodthirsty tyrant who put many Christians to death, quite possibly including Paul himself. Communism was an evil form of government, but when communism fell and the Soviet Union crumbled, the result was a period of anarchy which was even worse than what had gone before. Bad government, while not desirable, is better than no government at all.

Paul is careful to say, however, that the state is not the ultimate expression of God's will. The Christian's attitude toward it should be one of "respect" and "honor" (verse 7), not love or unquestioned obedience, as is the case with God. If the state departs from its proper goal of the betterment of all citizens, the Christian's responsibility is to urge it back along the right path. In a democracy, this means the believer has a strong responsibility to participate in the democratic process and not abstain from it. The governing authorities are subject to God, whether or not they acknowledge it, and the responsibility of the believer to submit to them is not on the same level as our responsibility to obey God. The state is not due any honor or respect because of some inherent quality it possesses, but only because the state has received its authority from God. The Christian citizen desires the good of the whole and is prepared to make sacrifices to that end, even if the state operates imperfectly, as it always does.

Paul's stress here is not on the degree to which governments may or may not be righteous, but on believers' obligation to restrict the outward exercise of their freedom in their civic responsibilities, so as to seek the well-being of others. In a democratic society at least, Christian citizens earn the praise of the authorities (and of God) not because of sheer unquestioning obedience, but because by their God-directed obedience they are acting in the best interests not only of themselves but also of their neighbors. Believers already following in the way of the cross should have a unique appreciation of the freedom they have to be able to lay down their rights joyously and voluntarily in such a manner. Christians should be the models of good citizenship in any society. But it is important to remember that Paul's interest here is in exhorting believers concerning the proper exercise of their freedom, not in expounding any particular understanding of the state.

The postmodern, post-Christian society in which we live is obsessed with rights. The reason is simple. It has lost sight of the Biblical truth that all people are made in the image of God, and are responsible to him to steward the life they have been given in obedience and faithfulness. They have no idea of the Biblical mandate to yield our rights if it is necessary for the well-being of others. Their goal is the promotion of their own interests, or that of the class or group with which they identify. The result is a collapse into the law of the jungle, where everyone competes for their piece of the pie, and those with the most power eventually triumph at the expense of the powerless and defenseless. Abortion is a case in point, but there are many others. It is understandable for those without any understanding of God to act like this, but it is disappointing when Christians are found among the groups loudly advocating for their own rights. Or even when Christians are advocating for rights which have more to do with their political or economic interests than with their Christian faith.

When government oversteps boundaries either by forbidding us to practice our faith, or by placing pressure on us to compromise our beliefs, we must respectfully refuse to obey and take the consequences. There is a role for legitimate civil disobedience, if its goal is not so much the advancement of our own rights as the protection of the rights of those who cannot defend themselves, or if its goal is the freedom to worship God and obey his law. History shows that a godly witness in the face of persecution is often the seedbed of revival. As the early church leader Tertullian said: "The blood of the martyrs is the seed of the church." The book of Revelation unfolds a scenario where satanic forces are continually attempting to pervert God's intention for civil government and turn it into an instrument of oppression. It does not suggest Christians engage in rebellion, but it does insist Christians refuse to compromise their faith, even at the cost of their lives. But the great message of Revelation is that God is on the throne. He is using even Satan's devices ultimately to further his rule, just as he did at the cross. And even if believers lose their lives, their heavenly reward far outweighs their earthly loss. Revelation presents the picture of suffering Christians as legal witnesses in a heavenly court where God uses that witness to bring judgment on those who have persecuted them. But our witness in the face of suffering may also be the very thing that draws people to Christ. Our witness, whether in a totalitarian state or in a democracy, is the most important asset we have.

In a democratic society, we are free to advocate for policies we believe are in line with Biblical principles. But the way we do so may make the difference between a fruitful witness and a big turn-off. The question in such circumstances is the state of our heart. Are we advocating for policies which will bring blessing to the society as a whole? Have we truly listened to the voices of those we disagree with and sought to understand them? Are we yelling at people or are we trying to win them over? Once an election is over, do we still have a relationship with our unsaved neighbors who voted differently? If not, then we have lost track of what God wants for us. The kingdom of God cannot be identified with any one political ideology. As Jesus told a worried Roman governor facing the prospect of insurrection, his kingdom is not of this world.

One thing is for sure. In any society, Christians should be the biggest peacemakers. Our faith is founded on reconciliation between God and humanity. As we model the life of the One who made that possible, we can bring reconciliation within communities and nations.

Let's use our political freedom wisely. It is not an end in itself. Its goal is the glory of God.

EIGHT

FREEDOM, THE WEAK
AND THE STRONG

13 Therefore let us not pass judgment on one another any longer, but rather decide never to put a stumbling block or hindrance in the way of a brother. 14 I know and am persuaded in the Lord Jesus that nothing is unclean in itself, but it is unclean for anyone who thinks it unclean. 15 For if your brother is grieved by what you eat, you are no longer walking in love. By what you eat, do not destroy the one for whom Christ died. (Rom. 14:13-15)

The church at Rome consisted of a majority of Gentiles and a minority of Jews. There was tension between the two groups. That is why in chapters 9-11, Paul addresses the relationship between Jews and Gentiles in the saving plan of God. From 14:1 to 15:7, he addresses a conflict between those described as "weak in faith" (14:1) and those described as "strong"

(15:1), a group Paul himself identifies with. Those pictured as weak observe certain days as special, and abstain from meat and wine (14:2, 5, 21). They are almost certainly Jewish converts to Christianity. Although the Old Testament did not prohibit the eating of all types of meat, it did prohibit some, and it would have been difficult or impossible for Jewish Christians to obtain kosher meat of any sort in Rome from their fellow Jews, who regarded them as heretics. And although the Old Testament prohibited only Nazirites from drinking wine, Jewish legalism may well have extended this prohibition with the result that Jewish Christians may have been total abstainers. Legalism and ascetic practices involving prohibition of certain food and drink were particularly common in Jewish communities outside Palestine. The Gentile majority in the church, by contrast, would see nothing wrong in drinking wine, or in eating non-kosher meat or even unclean meat like pork. The special days observed by the weak were probably Jewish feasts. Gentile members of the church would have had no interest in them at all. And so conflict arose.

Without doubt, the Gentile majority felt they had the perfect right to eat and drink whatever they wanted. Why should they observe Jewish feasts that had no relevance for them? They felt resentful that a Jewish minority were threatening their rights and their freedom. Theologically, Paul sides with the Gentiles. His view on food and drink is stated in verse 14a: "I know and am persuaded in the Lord Jesus that nothing is unclean in itself." After all, had Jesus not said the very same thing (Mk. 7:19)? Yet in the very next words, he turns everything upside down: "... but it is unclean for anyone who thinks it is unclean. For if your brother is grieved by what you eat, you are no longer walking in love" (verses 14b-15a). To walk in love means to refuse to exercise our own freedom in the greater good of caring for a weaker believer whose faith has not matured to the point where he can exercise the full freedom Christ has won for him. Something more important than the right to eat and drink what we want is at stake. If the exercise of freedom by the Gentiles is harmful to the weaker believers coming out of Judaism, even though the Gentiles are stronger in their faith and understanding, *and technically correct theologically*, it is their conduct that must change. The Gentile believers knew they were no longer under obligation to perform the ceremonial aspects of the law, including the observance of special days and the avoidance of food considered unclean. But if the full outward exercise of their inner Christian freedom caused such offence to the weaker believers that they left the church or engaged in actions they believed were offensive to God, they must lay that freedom down.

Indiscriminate exercise of freedom on the part of the strong could lead the weaker person into committing acts which he or she does not have the inner freedom in his faith to do. And so weaker believers wind up doing things they believe are offensive to the Lord, which for such persons constitute sin, as verse 23 makes clear: "For whoever has doubts is condemned if he eats, because the eating is not from faith. For whatever does not proceed from faith is sin." If such believers do something they believe is in disobedience to God, it is sin, even though the act of eating is not sinful in itself. It is a matter of the motivation of the heart. So for the strong to exercise their freedom without regard to the effect on the weak brings about the spiritual downfall of the weak. Paul puts this in the strongest possible language: we destroy those for whom Christ has died (verse 15b).

To be free from the old rituals is good, but to walk in love is better. It costs us nothing in terms of our true inner freedom, but it saves others from disaster. Paul walked this out in his own life. Though he considered himself free from the obligation to perform the ceremonial aspects of the law, yet when in Jerusalem he followed Jewish customs because he did not want to cause offence. No doubt the Jewish Christian community in Jerusalem had a lot to cope with, and did not want to offend their orthodox neighbors unnecessarily. For some of them, ritual observances were simply a part of their Jewish identity, even if not necessary for salvation. For others, such observances were still seen as expressions of obedience to God, again even if not necessary for salvation.

To fulfill God's law involves placing the good of our neighbor ahead of our own interest (Rom. 13:8-10). In terms of his personal convictions, Paul comes down on the side of the strong. Yet he himself is prepared to lead the way in renouncing the outward exercise of his freedom if such exercise is ruinous to the weak. Freedom is not an end in itself. It must be subject to love.

16 So do not let what you regard as good be spoken of as evil.

The strong are not to allow what they regard as good to be spoken of as evil. Their eating of all foods, drinking of wine and mocking the observance of special days has become the cause of division within the church by offending the weak. The weak are not the kind of Pharisaical legalists threatening the Galatian church. They are people who understand they are saved by grace, yet feel they must continue in certain Jewish observances in order not to offend the Lord.

17 For the kingdom of God is not a matter of eating and drinking but of righteousness and peace and joy in the Holy Spirit. 18 Whoever thus serves Christ is acceptable to God and approved by men. 19 So then let us pursue what makes for peace and for mutual upbuilding.

The next verses make clear the fact that the work of the Holy Spirit is to produce an environment of righteousness, peace and joy which results in the upbuilding of every member of the body. Pursuit by the strong of the rights they feel their freedom gives them works against the intentions of the Holy Spirit to produce peace and unity in the body.

20 Do not, for the sake of food, destroy the work of God. Everything is indeed clean, but it is wrong for anyone to make another stumble by what he eats. 21 It is good not to eat meat or drink wine or do anything that causes your brother to stumble. 22 The faith that you have, keep between yourself and God. Blessed is the one who has no reason to pass judgment on himself for what he approves.

In verse 20, Paul again addresses the strong believer: "Do not, for the sake of food, destroy the work of God." The wrong outward exercise of their inner freedom will bring destruction. In making the assertion "everything is indeed clean" Paul takes up the slogan of the strong, but then qualifies it: "but it is unclean for anyone who thinks it unclean." What is wrong is the outward expression of the genuine freedom attained in Christ where such expression causes injury to the weak person who has not yet fully comprehended or accepted that freedom. Yet love is not intended to lead us back into legalism. Legalism says that the weak believer who abstains from certain foods and drink is in the best spiritual place possible. True Christian freedom acknowledges it is the strong who have reached full understanding of what Christ did for us, but included in that freedom is the willingness to forego the exercise of it, if that is what is takes to protect the weaker believer from harm.

What advantage, then, is there to possessing a true understanding of freedom when you can't fully exercise that freedom? Strong believers have more freedom of action than the weak because they have the inner freedom to eat meat or drink wine, but they also have the freedom to refrain. Inner freedom is never lost. But the exercise of that freedom is always conditioned by the love that sent Christ to the cross and caused him to give up the freedom of eternal fellowship within the Trinity to humble himself and take on the form of a slave. The faith that the strong have is kept between themselves and the Lord, but they have no reason to pass judgment on themselves, for they have a clear conscience (verse 22). Freedom in Christ starts and ends in the hearts of believers and in their relationship with the Lord. It is not affected by what happens on the outside, whether having to put up with weaker believers or being thrown into prison. Paul experienced both, yet never lost his freedom. And there, in a nutshell, is the advantage of the strong.

23 But whoever has doubts is condemned if he eats, because the eating is not from faith. For whatever does not proceed from faith is sin.

The meaning of verse 23 is that weak believers are judged because they do what their faith, *according to their limited understanding of it,* forbids. This places them in conflict with what, *on their understanding,* is their commitment to Christ. Paul is dealing with the deep matters of the heart, not the externals of food and drink. Strong believers exercise their freedom on the basis of how it affects those who have not yet found that freedom, and they do so in hope that in time they will find it. But in the meantime, their wrong action might lead to the spiritual destruction of their brothers and sisters in Christ. And that is wrong.

A similar theme is explored from a different angle in 1 Cor. 8:7-13.

7 However, not all possess this knowledge. But some, through former association with idols, eat food as really offered to an idol, and their conscience, being weak, is defiled. 8 Food will not commend us to God. We are no worse off if we do not eat, and no better off if we do. 9 But take care that this right of yours does not somehow become a stumbling block to the weak. 10 For if anyone sees you who have knowledge eating in an idol's temple, will he not be encouraged, if his conscience is weak, to eat food offered to idols? 11 And so by your knowledge this weak person is destroyed, the brother for whom Christ died. 12 Thus, sinning against your brothers and wounding their conscience when it is weak, you sin against Christ. 13 Therefore, if food makes my brother stumble, I will never eat meat, lest I make my brother stumble.

The problem here starts with knowledge divorced from love. The "knowledge" referred to in verse 7 is the fact that idols have no true existence in themselves. This is a knowledge mature Christians in the church have arrived at, but it is not shared by immature believers still deeply affected by their previous experience as idol worshipers. In this case, unlike the situation in Rome, their concern is not with the type of food involved. It is with the fact that this food has been offered to idols, and hence in their view is spiritually defiled. And there is a further problem in that some believers have been seen eating this food in idol temples. As far as food is concerned, Paul takes the side of the strong believers, as he did in Rome: "We are no worse off if we do not eat, and no better off if we do" (verse 8). But then he gives a warning: the exercise of our freedom may become a stumbling block to the weak if they see us eating in an idol temple (verses 9-10). A freedom based on knowledge but isolated from love does not represent mature Christian conduct or a proper understanding of Christian freedom.

But what, we might ask, are Christians doing in an idol temple? The answer is that precincts of idol temples frequently included areas for commercial and social activity. They were the functional equivalent of our restaurants. Vast quantities of meat were dedicated to idols in the temple rituals, but never consumed. They were resold by the priests to commercial vendors, who then cooked and sold the food on the premises, or ran the equivalent of a butcher shop. It would have been practically impossible to avoid eating meat guaranteed never to have passed through an idol temple. The strong Christians pictured here were not engaging in idol worship, but merely visiting the butcher or having lunch out. But for the weak, the fact they were on location in an idol temple was a stumbling block. If they were pressured to eat the same meat or even come to the temple itself, it might cause the ruin of their faith by blurring the distinction between their new Christian faith and their old idolatrous practices. The result would be disastrous: "And so by your knowledge this weak person is destroyed, the brother for whom Christ died" (verse 11). So Paul can eat with perfect liberty as far as his own conscience is concerned. But if the exercise of his freedom causes a weaker person to stumble, he is willing never to eat meat again (verse 13).

Before he goes any further, Paul points to the example he has set in his own life. "Am I not free?" he declares (9:1). Is he not an apostle who has seen Jesus personally? Is the Corinthian church not a living proof of his credentials as a leader? And yet he refuses to exercise the rights his own life and ministry have given him. He serves at his own expense (verse 6). He has every right, according to the Scriptures, to claim an income from the Corinthians (verses 8-12a), but he refuses to exercise those rights because he does not want to put any obstacle in the way of people coming to Christ (verse 12b). There were many false spiritual leaders in the Greek world who made an income by preying on people, and Paul may have felt he had to avoid any appearance of money tainting his own ministry. The Lord commanded that those who proclaim the gospel should get their living from the gospel (verse 14), but he refuses to use this right (verse 15). He does not want anyone suggesting his motivation in preaching is financial reward, so he gives the gospel away free of charge and refuses to use the right he has, and that itself becomes his reward (verse 18). He has been teaching the strong believers at Corinth about giving up the outward exercise of their inner freedom. In this passage, he shows how he has set the example for them in his own life.

The next verses are significant, because they give the theological basis for the example Paul felt he needed to set:

19 For though I am free from all, I have made myself a servant to all, that I might win more of them. 20 To the Jews I became as a Jew, in order to win Jews. To those under the law I became as one under the law (though not being myself under the law) that I might win those under the law. 21 To those outside the law I became as one outside the law (not being outside the law of God but under the law of Christ) that I might win those outside the law. 22 To the weak I became weak, that I might win the weak. I have become all things to all people, that by all means I might save some. 23 I do it all for the sake of the gospel, that I may share with them in its blessings.

In verse 19, Paul returns to the theme of freedom he started with in verse 1. The basis of all his actions recorded in the intervening verses is explained by the principle that freedom in Christ is made real through serving others. The one who is truly free in Christ is ready to be a servant to all. Paul agrees that the strong believers are truly free, but he disagrees with the way they choose to exercise that freedom. His view of the way we should exercise freedom is anchored in his understanding of the way the Christian relates to the law. Even though he is willing to accommodate Jewish customs when with Jews, he himself is not under the old dietary and ritual purity aspects of the law (verse 20), for Christ has purified us by his one perfect sacrifice. But this does not mean that Paul simply threw the law out the window. He reminds the Gentile believers that he is not "outside the law of God but under the law of Christ" (verse 21). His relationship to the law has changed. He no longer pursues obedience to the law in order to gain acceptance by God, but he is still committed to obedience to the law though his relationship to Christ. *He relates to the law through Christ.* There are two mistakes we can make in relation to the law. We can regard it as a means of salvation, or we can discard it entirely. Both are wrong. *We obey the law through the framework of our justification by faith.* As we saw in previous chapters, we no longer need to fulfil the ceremonial and ritual purity aspects of the law, which are expressions of the old sacrificial system, but we are still bound by the heart or moral dimension of the law, which commands love for God and neighbor. It is why Jesus and the early church set such a high standard when it came to things like the sanctity of marriage. The writers of the New Testament letters, as we have pointed out previously, did not just make up their lists of moral commands. They were simply teaching the moral principles laid down in the Old Testament.

Why this is such an important principle for us today is the postmodern emphasis on an undefined concept of love. Postmodern theologians tell us the "law of Christ" is the new way of "love." This is then defined as a substitute for the old way of defined moral commands that characterized the law. Those commands, in their opinion, are nothing more than outdated cultural concepts. What is important now, they say, is unconditional love and acceptance. We must avoid any form of judgment based on defined standards of right and wrong. But that is not what Paul refers to in verse 21 as the "law of Christ." As we explained in chapter six, the law of Christ is the Old Testament law properly interpreted and understood. Its sacrificial dimension is ended, but its moral law still applies, and is the basis for all Jesus' teaching on righteous conduct. And Jesus' teaching is the foundation on which Paul undoubtedly built.

Paul is prepared (verses 22-23) to sacrifice the outward exercise of his inner freedom whenever it is necessary to obtain the salvation of others and strengthen their faith in Christ. This he sees as true obedience to the command of the law to love God and neighbor.

Paul concludes his discussion in 1 Corinthians 10:14-22.

14 Therefore, my beloved, flee from idolatry. 15 I speak as to sensible people; judge for yourselves what I say. 16 The cup of blessing that we bless, is it not a participation in the blood of Christ? The bread that we break, is it not a participation in the body of Christ? 17 Because there is one bread, we who are many are one body, for we all partake of the one bread. 18 Consider the people of Israel: are not those who eat the sacrifices participants in the altar? 19 What do I imply then? That food offered to idols is anything, or that an idol is anything? 20 No, I imply that what pagans sacrifice they offer to demons and not to God. I do not want you to be participants with demons. 21 You cannot drink the cup of the Lord and the cup of demons. You cannot partake of the table of the Lord and the table of demons. 22 Shall we provoke the Lord to jealousy? Are we stronger than he?

In chapter 8, Paul referred to two situations. The first was the purchase of meat previously offered to idols from a butcher who doubled as a temple employee. The second was a social function in which a banquet was held in the precincts of the temple. Ancient documents refer to such events. In effect, as we pointed out above, the temple served as a kind of restaurant. In either case, the believer is free to eat or drink because no food is unclean. But that freedom must not be exercised if our eating causes weaker believers to stumble by eating what they regard as forbidden. Now it seems another situation is involved. Some believers are going beyond simply eating in the idol temple. They feel free, while on the premises, to participate in idolatrous rituals on the grounds that the idols don't really exist. Even though idols have no reality in themselves, Paul points out, they do represent demonic entities opposed to God, which is why God forbade all forms of idolatry in the law. This abuse of freedom goes beyond the previous form, and invites destruction not only for the weak, but also for the strong. The strong believers in Corinth were in danger of so exalting their own freedom as an end in itself that some of them at least were in danger of disowning the One from whom that freedom had come. A contemporary example might be Christians who not only drink alcohol but abuse it, or Christians who enjoy entertainment but allow themselves to view morally questionable forms of it. This shows once again that freedom in itself is not the highest goal of the Christian life, nor a goal to be pursued independent of our following Jesus in the way of the cross.

23 "All things are lawful," but not all things are helpful. "All things are lawful," but not all things build up. 24 Let no one seek his own good, but the good of his neighbor. 25 Eat whatever is sold in the meat market without raising any question on the ground of conscience. 26 For "the earth is the Lord's, and the fullness thereof." 27 If one of the unbelievers invites you to dinner and you are disposed to go, eat whatever is set before you without raising any question on the ground of conscience. 28 But if someone says to you, "This has been offered in sacrifice," then do not eat it, for the sake of the one who informed you, and for the sake of conscience— 29 I do not mean your conscience, but his. For why should my liberty be determined by someone else's conscience? 30 If I partake with thankfulness, why am I denounced because of that for which I give thanks?

The strong believers declare: "All things are lawful" (verse 23). Paul responds by saying: "Not all things build up." He returns to the theme of the fulfilling of the law he has set forth in Rom. 13:8-10. No one is to seek his own good, but that of his neighbor (verse 24). But then he underlines the legitimate freedom won by Christ. The believer may eat anything sold in the meat market without raising any questions of conscience. Quoting Ps. 24:1, he roots his teaching squarely in the Old Testament: "The earth is the Lord's, and the fullness thereof" (verses 25-26). Similarly, one may go to dinner at the home of an unbeliever, and eat anything that is offered. However, if someone else is present (presumably a weak believer) and points out that the meat had been sacrificed to idols, they must again give up the exercise of their freedom (verses 27-28). Paul is careful to add that his own inner freedom is not compromised by his willingness to refrain from exercising it outwardly, for why should his freedom be determined by someone else's weak conscience (verse 29)?

31 So, whether you eat or drink, or whatever you do, do all to the glory of God. 32 Give no offense to Jews or to Greeks or to the church of God, 33 just as I try to please everyone in everything I do, not seeking my own advantage, but that of many, that they may be saved.

The ultimate goal of all our actions is the glory of God. The immediate goal is the spiritual well-being of those around us. The exercise of our freedom is to be guided by what will best serve those two goals. This has many applications in our own church culture. An obvious one is the use of alcohol. Alcohol is not evil in itself, or Jesus would scarcely have changed water into wine (although what we understand as wine today is considerably stronger than what was on offer at the wedding Jesus was attending). But there are many who come to faith from a background in various forms of addictions. For them to see a mature believer drinking alcohol might cause them to feel they can do so themselves, which could then lead to disaster. We must walk a fine line between limiting the outward exercise of our legitimate inner freedom in the interest of weak believers, and giving in to straight-out legalism. A mature, Spirit-led church culture will find a way. It may well be that in the process the weak are led to a place of greater strength, at least to the point where someone else exercising their freedom is not a stumbling block to them. We need to bear in mind, however, that we live in a very broken culture, and we can expect a steady stream of broken people to come into our churches. These are the weak, and to disciple them into strength will require great sensitivity to their needs. A truly strong church will rise to the occasion.

This concept of freedom is the polar opposite of the self-fulfillment posture so prevalent in our pagan culture. It is a tragedy when this mentality comes into the church. A proper understanding of Christian freedom will prevent that from happening. No matter how dark the world is around us, we can still be salt and light in it. Christians who clamor for their own rights without regard for the effect on those weaker in maturity and understanding are in danger of being salt that has lost its usefulness and no longer good for anything (Mt. 5:13). Perhaps that is one of the many reasons why the church in our contemporary culture has lost much of its power.

NINE

FREEDOM, RACE, AND SLAVERY

The Corinthians lived in the midst of the ancient Greek fate-based honor and shame culture we talked about at the beginning of this book. A person's worth was determined by outward appearance, and so money and social status meant everything. And this was a real issue in a society where a substantial proportion of the population were slaves, even though the Greek institution of slavery was nothing like its modern racially-based version. Freedom was possessed by those at the top of the social structure. The greatest goal of many slaves was to attain that freedom. When the message of the Gospel entered this culture, it challenged its values to the core, and eventually undermined the institution of slavery. Yet Christ did not come to initiate a social or political revolution. How did Paul teach the real meaning of freedom to a culture which (like ours) saw freedom in a much different light? Our first stop is at 1 Corinthians 7.

17 Only let each person lead the life that the Lord has assigned to him, and to which God has called him. This is my rule in all the churches. 18 Was anyone at the time of his call already circumcised? Let him not seek to remove the marks of circumcision. Was anyone at the time of his call uncircumcised? Let him not seek circumcision. 19 For neither circumcision counts for anything nor uncircumcision, but keeping the commandments of God. 20 Each one should remain in the condition in which he was called.

The thrust of Paul's teaching here is that the circumstances of a person's outward status cannot affect their freedom in Christ. A Christian does not have to attain a certain outward situation in life in order to be truly free or to serve God effectively. Elsewhere he has taught that God has given to each person a measure of faith (Rom. 12:3), a ministry (1 Cor. 3:5) and various spiritual gifts (1 Cor. 12:7). Here he says that God has also apportioned to each person a situation in life to which he has called them. The Lord has assigned this situation just as much as he has assigned a ministry or spiritual gift. So we should not feel under pressure to seek freedom from the social or outward circumstances in which we find ourselves. We have already found true freedom in Christ, and we need to know how to work out that freedom in the situation God has placed us in.

This puts Christianity in radical opposition to the postmodern culture in which we live, where people are encouraged to seek self-fulfillment and personal freedom by enlarging their spheres of liberty at the expense of others. That is the essence of social justice or critical theory. It also puts Christianity at odds with traditional liberalism, which has emphasized freedom as the highest value of all. This does not mean that Christianity opposes political freedom. Far from it. Christians should always be in the forefront of the struggle for greater freedoms, because Christianity above all other faiths places a high value on the worth of each person on the planet, no matter what their beliefs. What a Biblical understanding of freedom does teach us, however, is that there is a deeper freedom no outward oppression can take away. And this freedom will carry us into a truly free eternity, whereas merely political or social freedom carries no such reward. Christians in the western world who complain about minor losses of freedom have lost sight of the fact that they are in a small minority in the body of Christ. Most Christians today live in societies where freedom is not valued as a basic human right, and thus they stand in great need of the assurance the Bible brings us that true freedom is God-given and cannot be taken away by any human power. Even martyrdom is the gateway to glory.

Believing as he does in the sovereignty of God, Paul confidently asserts that God has called us into the situation in life in which we are placed (verse 17). Up until now in this chapter (verses 1-16), he has talked about marital freedom in relation to various groups: those who are married, those who are celibate, those who are widows or widowers, and those who are separated. These we discuss in the next chapter. But in this section, his focus is racial and social. How do we understand freedom in relation to those born Jew or Gentile, and those born slave or free?

First, he addresses the issue of those born circumcised. All the male Jewish converts in the church were circumcised. Yet here he must urge these men not to seek to remove the sign of circumcision (verse 18). Greek men exercised naked — the word gymnasium is derived from the Greek word *gumnos,* meaning naked. The gymnasium was a common place for men to congregate, probably even more than it is today. Without putting matters too bluntly, it was rapidly obvious who was circumcised and who was not. Circumcision was a matter of ridicule as far as the pagan society was concerned, and many Jewish men sought a surgical procedure which removed its appearance. The fact that so many sought such a delicate, painful and possibly dangerous procedure is a testimony to the shame associated with circumcision. Paul is clear. Don't do it! You don't need to do it because the status you have in Christ is far greater and more elevated than any further measure of acceptance you would gain from (for instance) pagan men at the gym. It's interesting that Paul's thinking here takes such a different tack from Galatians, where he exercises a lot of energy attacking the people urging believers to get circumcised. But the underlying principle is the same: "For neither circumcision counts for anything nor uncircumcision, but keeping the commandments of God" (verse 19). Of course, the Jew would say that circumcision was a commandment of God, but Paul understood that we are no longer obligated to follow the ceremonial aspects of the law, those aspects which were particularly designed to guide the national life of a people and ended through the sacrifice of Christ. Now in Christ, God's covenant has been widened to include people of every nation, and so circumcision no longer has value as far as salvation is concerned. Yet circumcision is part of the life situation the Jewish male convert to Christ finds himself in, and as such he is just to accept it, as it has no bearing on his Christian freedom, or on the worth and value he has found in Christ.

21 Were you a bondservant when called? Do not be concerned about it. (But if you can gain your freedom, avail yourself of the opportunity.) 22 For he who was called in the Lord as a bondservant is a freedman of the Lord. Likewise he who was free when called is a bondservant of Christ. 23 You were bought with a price; do not become bondservants of men. 24 So, brothers, in whatever condition each was called, there let him remain with God.

Paul next turns to another significant life situation, that of being a free person or a slave. In verse 21, he addresses the Christian slaves: "Were you a bondservant when called? Do not be concerned about it." The idea is the same as with circumcision: the outward situation of life in which we find ourselves is entirely secondary to our calling as Christians and to true Christian freedom, which is unaffected by legal or social status. The second half of the verse, literally translated, is "Even if you can gain your freedom, rather make use of..." Paul leaves hanging what it is we are to make use of. The ESV assumes it is freedom, hence the translation, "But if you can gain your freedom, avail yourself of the opportunity." Other scholars have proposed the idea that the unspoken word here is not "freedom," but "slavery." This yields the translation, "Even if you can gain your freedom, make use of the situation of slavery in which you find yourself." Against this it is argued how could anyone *make use of* such a situation, one which is hopeless and in which one has no choices to begin with? But this is to misunderstand the Greco-Roman institution of slavery, which was nothing like its horrendous modern equivalent (see further in the next section). Often freed people were in worse economic circumstances than slaves in a prosperous household.

The best translation is one in line with the context. Paul has argued it doesn't matter what your circumstances are when you came to Christ, just make the best use of what God has placed in front of you. Christians are to accept the situation they are in, rather than trying to change it. Hence we should translate the verse, "Even if you can gain your freedom, make use of the situation [of slavery] God has placed you in." If you are a slave, serve Christ as a slave. Paul is not forbidding Christian slaves to take the opportunity of becoming free persons; he is simply telling them to find God in the situation. If God opens the door to freedom, then by all means take it (verse 20b), but don't make that your primary goal in life.

Paul told the circumcised males to make use of their situation, rather than trying to gain social acceptance by having their circumcision reversed. Now he is telling slaves something similar. If they are freed, well and good, but even if they are not, they can still serve Christ. At the heart of all this is Paul's understanding of true freedom. When we come to Christ, we are freed from the ownership of Satan and placed in God's family. That is true freedom. That is the highest standing we could ever attain. The slave's standing depended on where he stood in the household of his master. Through faith in Christ, we have been placed in God's own household, no longer as slaves but as sons and daughters. There is no higher standing than what we already have.

FREEDOM, SLAVES AND MASTERS (GAL. 6:5-9)

5 "Bondservants, obey your earthly masters with fear and trembling, with a sincere heart, as you would Christ, 6 not by the way of eye-service, as people-pleasers, but as bondservants of Christ, doing the will of God from the heart, 7 rendering service with a good will as to the Lord and not to man,"

Slavery in the Greco-Roman world was not the same as our picture of slavery. It was not based on race, for one thing. You could sell yourself into slavery in order to get a better job or even improve your social standing. Many slaves were trained professionally and became teachers, physicians or business managers in the master's household. You could even sell yourself into slavery for a limited period of time and then become a free person again. Slaves often enjoyed what we would call "employee benefit packages," including housing and health care. Their owner had obligations to provide for them. Sometimes, in fact, masters freed slaves because they did not want to carry the economic cost. Having said that, masters could be cruel and the rights of slaves were limited. Much depended on your personal circumstances and abilities, and the type of household in which you were a slave. One practical application of this is that much of what Paul writes here can without too much difficulty be translated into our present-day categories of employers and employees.

What is interesting here is the way Paul starts. He does so by addressing the slaves. A Roman writer who was a citizen, like Paul, would never have lowered himself to addressing slaves in a letter like this. But they were part of the church to which Paul was writing, and he addresses them because to him they are Christians before they are slaves. As he wrote to the Galatians, in Christ there is no slave or free. Paul did not directly advocate the abolition of slavery, but the logic of his thinking and conduct led Christians though the ages to see slavery, particularly in its modern, racialized form, as something abhorrent and incompatible with the Gospel.

Yet slaves are instructed to obey their masters (verse 5). Their outward freedom is restricted by their social and economic circumstances, and this is a reflection of life in a fallen world. Paul recognizes that God has placed order in the midst of a broken world for a reason, and the reason is to protect people from the consequences of anarchy. This does not mean that God endorses a particular form of social organization, nor that Christians are forbidden from seeking better forms than currently prevail. Modern history provides countless examples of Christians seeking better order in the societies in which they live. Our primary goal should be the placing of value on each and every person. Christian slaves lived in a world of outwardly restricted freedom, yet the answer to such restriction was not a rebellion which might result in chaos or even worse repression. Their true inner freedom rooted in their identity in Christ allowed Christian slaves to live in peace within a system that restricted their outward liberty. Even imperfect order is better than no order, and God has allowed this order to take place.

Slavery in Paul's world, as mentioned above, did often provide a net benefit to those who were slaves. Paul is not commissioned by God to untangle the social web of society, but to teach Christians how to conduct themselves in the midst of it. Slaves are to obey "with fear and trembling" and a "sincere heart." The same word "fear" is used of wives in 5:33, but translated "respect." Whether respect or fear, the slave's obedience is rooted and grounded in one significant phrase, "as you would Christ." The master ultimately deserves respect *only because Christ has allowed him to occupy that position.* Because it is Christ who is the real object of our obedience, slaves are called to obey masters whether they are Christians or not. It is not because a master is a Christian that he is to be obeyed, but because God has allowed him to have that place. If everyone plays their part properly, everyone will benefit. It is important to remember that God did not design human society with slavery in mind. Society was corrupted when the first individuals fell. In the midst of a fallen world, God mercifully intervenes in the society of the day to establish an order which is designed to be protective rather than damaging, even though it is not perfect.

In verses 6-7, Paul elaborates on this theme. Slaves are to serve "as bondservants [slaves] of Christ, doing the will of God from the heart, rendering service with a good will as to the Lord and not to man." It is not their master who has earned the right to their service. It is Christ. It is ultimately the Lord who is to be pleased, not their master. Their fundamental identity is therefore as slaves of Christ, not of man. When the slave finds his or her identity in Christ, they find themselves as followers of the One who, though he was God, came to earth in the form of a slave (Phil 2:7). They discover as Christians that they have the same level of worth, value and identity as a believing master who, though free, is at a deeper level a slave of Christ, for "he who was free when called is a bondservant [slave] of Christ" (1 Cor. 7:22). Slaves find themselves following in the footsteps of the One who, knowing that the Father had put all things into his hands, took the towel, poured water into a basin and began to wash the disciple's feet (Jn. 13:3-5). With these words in verses 6-7, Paul relativizes the social institution of slavery in the Greco-Roman world (along with every other historical form of slavery), and fundamentally undermines it by declaring the equal worth and value of each person. Later the Holy Spirit would use other Christians such as William Wilberforce and Martin Luther King to undertake the practical outworking of Paul's theological truth. Paul is speaking into a social order he is not empowered by God to change. Yet his words bring a freedom to the heart and soul of Christian slaves, and lift them out of the sense of being property rather than people. It's not hard to find an application for Christian employees today.

8 knowing that whatever good anyone does, this he will receive back from the Lord, whether he is a bondservant or is free.

And there is a reward from the Lord for believers who act rightly, whether they are slaves or free. The reward may well come in the future — quite often it will only come in eternity. But it will come. Jesus told a parable of a beggar and a rich man in which their positions were reversed in the eternal kingdom. We find this difficult to comprehend because, especially in our western materialistic society, we are so focused on what we can see, touch and feel around us, the things that Paul said elsewhere were passing away. But for the believer, death is the gateway to an eternity for which this life is only a preparation. This does not mean Christians should overlook injustice in this world. Far from it. But it does mean that, even where it is not in our power to change things in this life, God can change them in eternity.

And whatever reward there is in eternity, the kingdom always comes in the form of the already-not yet. The kingdom is present, even though not in its fulfilled form. There is a reward even in this life for those who obey. We reap what we sow in this present life. Jesus demonstrated that the way to exaltation was humiliation. For a slave to obey an unbelieving master and do so from the heart seems a losing proposition. Yet what alternative does he have, other than to obey grudgingly or in anger? But to invest in obedience releases the power of God to act on our behalf. Even in this life we can reap the fruit of obedience. At the very moment we are most powerless to act for ourselves, we may well find God acting for us. I have often seen God intervene on behalf of a Christian employee facing possible injustice, and even as I write these words I am involved in another such situation.

The nature of slavery in the world to which Paul was writing does make it possible to draw parallels to the employer-employee relationship as we experience it today. Employees are called to submit to their employers, whether they are believers or not, and to serve willingly and with a good heart. God has placed an order in society for the greater good. It may be corrupted by those who hold power, but it is still better than anarchy, which is no order at all. In general, and especially in the free societies in which most of us are privileged to live, it is for the good of all for employees to serve the larger good of the employer, who then prospers and is able to reward employees for their labor. Paul is not writing a handbook on social or political activism, and neither am I. He is dealing with matters of the heart and our relationship with the Lord, and with consequences which will last through eternity. If we get these things right, we may well find the Lord will fight our cause in this life more effectively than we ever could.

9 Masters, do the same to them, and stop your threatening, knowing that he who is both their Master and yours is in heaven, and that there is no partiality with him."

In the context of a pagan culture where slavery was widespread and there was a great divide between masters and slaves, Paul's words are revolutionary. Contrary to the thinking of the ancient world, masters (if they are Christians) are not free to do what they want with their slaves. They are to "do the same to them." In other words, they are to treat their slaves with respect, care, sincerity and goodwill. Their commitment to Christ brings fundamental change to the way masters are to act toward their slaves. It restricts their freedom, for now they must always be conscious of their slaves' welfare. Masters often operated by instilling fear in their slaves, but Paul commands them to stop their threatening. Implicit in this is the thought that they are to trust the Lord that their slaves will continue to perform their duties even if they are not being harassed and intimidated.

Why masters must not intimidate is made clear: God is Master of both slave and free, and equally so, for there is no special treatment of masters with the Lord. In the parallel passage in Col. 3:25, Paul tells the slaves they will be judged impartially for wrongdoing, and here he tells the masters the same thing. Masters are subject to the requirement of God's law that they love their neighbor as themselves, and their Christian freedom can only operate within these limits. With these words Paul sounded the eventual virtual death-knell of the institution of slavery in the Roman and post-Roman world.

Paul's direction to the churches must have caused many in pagan society to think of him as a dangerous social radical, and of course the Gospel is revolutionary in its implications. Paul was not overthrowing the system; that was not his mandate from God. But he was bringing a reform to the system that, in grounding the relationship between master and slave in the requirements of God's law to love one another and place the interest of the other ahead of one's own, could not but lead Christians of later generations to conclude that slavery, in whatever form it took, was wrong.

The threat Paul's understanding of freedom poses to the institution of slavery does not come from a condemnation of slavery as such (though neither does he approve of it), nor from an interest in the attainment of freedom as an end in itself (which would ultimately prove self-seeking and a doorway to the abuse of the rights of others). Rather, the threat comes from his command for both masters and slaves to allow their conduct to be subject to the lordship of Christ and their relationships to be cemented by the bond of love (Col. 3:14). This amounts to a restriction on the exercise of freedom by both groups, and so hits at the very underpinnings of the institution of slavery, which is based on the right of unrestricted exercise of liberty by the one group at the expense of the liberty of the other. The eventual results of Paul's teaching are foreshadowed in Philemon, where Paul appeals to Philemon to welcome back Onesimus, his runaway slave, no longer as a slave but as a brother (Philemon verse 16).

Even though we do not live in a society which practices or condones slavery, we do live in a world of employers and employees. Christian employees should be honest, hard-working and concerned for the prosperity of the businesses for which they work. Christian employers should place the welfare of their employees before the cause of making ever-increasing amounts of profit. Is it not possible, one may ask, that in a business where both employees and employers conducted themselves like this, the net result would be benefit to all? That would be a sign that the kingdom of God has come to the business world. Or, for that matter, to the public sector, where the same principles apply, even though the profit motive is absent. God has designed his kingdom to operate in all spheres of society. In the words of the great theologian-politician Abraham Kuyper: "There is not one square inch of this earth over which Christ does not cry, "Mine!"

TEN

FREEDOM, SEX AND MARRIAGE

1 Now concerning the matters about which you wrote: "It is good for a man not to have sexual relations with a woman." 2 But because of the temptation to sexual immorality, each man should have his own wife and each woman her own husband. (1 Cor. 7:1-2)

Paul has received a series of questions from the Corinthian church. This explains his opening words: "Now concerning the matters about which you wrote" (verse 1). This is the first of a number of questions Paul answers in this letter. Others include "Now concerning the betrothed" (7:25); "Now concerning food offered to idols" (8:1); and "Now concerning spiritual gifts" (12:1). These questions arose out of internal dissensions in the church. From time to time Paul quotes slogans promoted by various congregational factions. The first of these appears in verse 1: "It is good for a man not to have sexual relations with a woman." It's important to understand this is not Paul's opinion; it's actually a view he is opposing.

A party within the Corinthian church had adopted the views of pagan philosophers concerning abstinence from sexual activity, even within marriage. This view is related to the Greek idea that the material realm is inferior to the spiritual and is of no importance. This led some people to feel they could engage in any kind of sexual activity they wanted, and others by contrast to avoid sexual activity altogether.

There were certainly people within the church who fell into the first category, but this group fell into the second. They thought that even married couples should have freedom not to engage in sexual relations if they didn't want to. They portrayed this as a more spiritual course of action. Paul's response to this begins in verse 2: "But because of the temptation to sexual immorality, each man should have his own wife and each woman her own husband." Paul approves of a healthy sexual relationship within marriage. This is counter-cultural not only to the ascetic view that sexual relations are wrong, but also to the general Roman view that the purpose of marriage is convenience — to produce an heir so that the estate is saved. Marriages often ended once the heir was produced, and divorce and infidelity were commonplace. The phrase "temptation to sexual immorality" represents the Greek word porneia, which refers to immoral sexual activity. It is used in the plural here, and is almost certainly a reference to some of the immoral sexual activities that have been going on in the Corinthian church as described in the preceding two chapters (men having sex with their father's wives and with prostitutes, and carrying on homosexual activities). Christians are not free to engage in any such relationships. The answer to these temptations to immorality is to have a good sexual relationship within the marriage covenant. Ancient Greek and Roman literature records the sad but familiar record of a double standard, with men having numerous extra-marital affairs while demanding their wives remain faithful. For Paul, the choices are either monogamy or celibacy. We are free to marry or not to marry, but we are not free to have sex outside of marriage.

3 The husband should give to his wife her conjugal rights, and likewise the wife to her husband. 4 For the wife does not have authority over her own body, but the husband does. Likewise the husband does not have authority over his own body, but the wife does.

In verses 3-4 Paul insists, against the standards of the day, that men are as bound as women to the marriage covenant. Neither husband nor wife has exclusive rights over their own body. Their freedom in relation to sex is limited by the presence of their spouse. And this is a mutual and equal obligation. Paul is not interested in the issue of rights, except to point out that our rights (or freedoms) are limited by the overriding obligation to fulfill the law's requirement that we love our neighbor, who in this case is our spouse. Christian marriage is grounded in the love of Christ.

5 Do not deprive one another, except perhaps by agreement for a limited time, that you may devote yourselves to prayer; but then come together again, so that Satan may not tempt you because of your lack of self-control. 6 Now as a concession, not a command, I say this.

The next statement introduces an exception: the husband and wife may agree to abstain from sexual relations temporarily in order to devote themselves to prayer. This abstaining from sex could be considered as a form of fasting. But Paul allows this only as a concession (verse 6). He is not giving a command that couples should engage in such abstinence, even for the purposes of prayer. His main point is that sexual relationships should be carried on in marriage, and only halted for a season (and if the couple both agree to do so) for purposes of prayer. *The concession of verse 6 applies only to the statement of verse 5 about times of prayer*, not the general statement about marriage in verses 2-4. In that case, Paul would be saying he *endorses sexual relationships within marriage only as a concession*, as if to say marriage without sex would be better. His statement about the concession refers grammatically to *what he has just said*, which is the idea of a temporary separation for the purpose of prayer. Paul would not urge sexual abstinence within marriage, for sexual union within marriage is an ordinance given by God (Gen. 2:24-25).

Paul needed to address the issue because of two reasons. First, some in the the Corinthian church felt their freedom in Christ extended to violating God's law as it pertains to the marriage covenant. They felt they could have sex in any circumstances and with anyone they wanted. Second, as mentioned above, some in the pagan culture looked down on sexual relationships as unnecessary and inferior. Further, this suited many people, for in the wider context of the Greco-Roman world, marriage was often a social sham. People got married for reasons of upward mobility, respectability, or the need to produce an heir. Many of these marriages were devoid of love, and ended when their benefits were no longer needed. There was no sex within marriage, but much sex outside of it. Against this, Paul both denies freedom to have sex outside the marriage covenant, and reaffirms the importance of sexual union within that covenant.

7 I wish that all were as I myself am. But each has his own gift from God, one of one kind and one of another. 8 To the unmarried and the widows I say that it is good for them to remain single, as I am. 9 But if they cannot exercise self-control, they should marry. For it is better to marry than to burn with passion.

Paul wishes that everyone were as he is, but says that each must live according to the gift God has given him (verse 7). He classifies himself in verse 8 as part of the group of "unmarried and widows." Most scholars take "unmarried" here to mean "widowers," to match with the mention of widows (there was a separate Greek word for "widower," but it was rarely used). This means Paul was actually a widower. This makes sense, for Paul deals later in the chapter with the different situation of people who have never yet married, but these comments are directed specifically to widows and widowers, not to the never married. It would have been very difficult for him to have attained the prominence he had within Pharisaic circles without ever having been married. Given that the average life expectancy of a woman in the Roman Empire was less than thirty years old (often due to complications in childbirth), it would not be at all surprising for Paul to have been widowed, and perhaps have lost both his wife and child in the process. His wish that all would be as he is must be understood in light of his comments later in the chapter about the troubles of the day in which he lived (verse 29), which meant that the responsibilities of marriage and family could well prove extremely challenging, and certainly in the situation of someone like Paul with his itinerant ministry and long periods of incarceration for the sake of the gospel. What this means for the never-married Christian's freedom to marry we will consider below in our comments on verse 29. But Paul's wish here for those who have lost a spouse to remain in that state is just that — a wish, not a command.

Paul is certainly not opposed to marriage. In fact, he is saying here that marriage is a gift (charisma) from God, as is celibacy. The two gifts are not simply celibacy and marriage, but the *ability to live celibate without continual emotional and physical frustration*, and the ability *to live in a married state and fulfill the responsibilities of marriage while serving the Lord*. But if Paul is in fact referring here to *widows and widowers*, all he is doing (in wishing all would remain as he is), is urging caution in rushing into *remarriage*. This caution turns out to be wise in light of what we now know about social life in the Roman Empire. There was enormous pressure on women to remarry and thus to secure greater social respectability and financial security. Widows were expected to remarry within a year, and divorcées within six months. Men were also caught up in this pressure. It was important to secure heirs for one's estate. Marriage might lead to financial improvement for men as well as women. It was not socially respectable to remain unmarried — even if the marriage was nothing more than one of convenience, and sexual activity (of all types) outside of marriage continued. Understanding the sanctity and seriousness of Christian marriage leads Paul to counsel against such marriages of convenience.

10 To the married I give this charge (not I, but the Lord): the wife should not separate from her husband 11 (but if she does, she should remain unmarried or else be reconciled to her husband), and the husband should not divorce his wife.

Paul next turns to the case of Christians already married but considering divorce. It turns out this is another situation where following Christ and obeying God's law limits our freedom of action. What is significant to begin with are the equal grounds on which Paul puts men and women. Neither men nor women are permitted simply to walk out of a marriage and enter into a new one. This is an enormous contrast to Judaism, where it is generally thought that only men could initiate divorce. Jesus did speak of a situation where a woman was divorcing her husband (Mk. 10:11-12), but he may have been referring to what was allowed under Roman law rather than Jewish law. The stricter Jews said that a man could divorce his wife only on grounds of unchastity, whereas the more liberally-minded Rabbis said a man could divorce his wife for whatever reason he wanted, even if, for instance, she had made a mess of dinner! Divorce and remarriage were extremely common in the Roman world, where both men and women walked in and out of marriages with great regularity. It was a common joke that certain women changed husbands with every passing year. Divorce consisted of one spouse simply telling the other to take their things and go. So for Paul to counsel against divorce was revolutionary in light of the wider social context, and for him to place men and women on equal grounds in this respect was revolutionary in the specifically Jewish context. Marriage is a part of God's law, and has been so since Genesis. We are not free to break the marriage covenant, and we should not enter the marriage covenant merely for reasons of convenience or comfort. It is a solemn and life-long commitment before God. As such, it is a God-appointed source of incomparable blessing and at the same time a serious restriction on our sexual and relational freedom.

It appears that Jesus took the side of the stricter Jews, at least on this topic, allowing for divorce only on the grounds of sexual unfaithfulness (Mt. 19:9). No doubt Paul was aware of this exception, but wanted to put more emphasis on the rule than the exception here in light of the battle he was fighting in relation to the very low view of marriage in the church in Corinth.

12 To the rest I say (I, not the Lord) that if any brother has a wife who is an unbeliever, and she consents to live with him, he should not divorce her. 13 If any woman has a husband who is an unbeliever, and he consents to live with her, she should not divorce him. 14 For the unbelieving husband is made holy because of his wife, and the unbelieving wife is made holy because of her husband. Otherwise your children would be unclean, but as it is, they are holy. 15 But if the unbelieving partner separates, let it be so. In such cases the brother or sister is not enslaved. God has called you to peace. 16 For how do you know, wife, whether you will save your husband? Or how do you know, husband, whether you will save your wife?

Paul was a busy pastor and he was dealing with all sorts of problems, just as pastors do today. Next on his agenda is the case of believers married to unbelievers. These are marriages entered into by two unbelievers, one of whom later became a Christian. The concern that is raised in verses 12-16 is from the viewpoint of a member of the church: does the presence of an unbelieving spouse bring spiritual danger into my home and to my children? And am I free now to separate or divorce? Paul's answer is as follows. If the unbelieving spouse is happy to continue with the marriage, the believer is not free to consider divorce (verses 12-13). The reason given for this is that the unbelieving spouse is "made holy" because of the believer (verse 14a). Paul's statement here has caused much puzzlement, mainly because the phrase "made holy" has been equated with being saved or being sanctified, and the conclusion appears to be that the unbeliever is saved simply by continuing in the marriage. Yet such a thought would be a total contradiction to everything Paul teaches on the nature of salvation, so we need to rethink what he is actually saying.

The theme of the paragraph has to do with relationships, the relationships between two spouses and the relationships between both of them and their children. In this passage we find a meaning of "holy" which is different from its normal use in the Bible. The word "holy" carries a range of meanings, all of which are rooted in the idea of God being completely different from us in the essence of who he is. To be holy means to carry something of the character of God. The idea of sanctification expresses the intention of God for Christian believers to have such a change of conduct by the working of the Spirit that they begin to look more like the God who created them and less like the fallen world in which they live. But we all know unbelievers can carry a measure of what we would call good character (which is God's character) within them. A person can have some good moral characteristics without being saved. Here, Paul speaks of unbelieving spouses who show an openness to God and a loving attitude by desiring to stay with the marriage covenant even when their spouse becomes a Christian — which is not, after all, what they signed on for. This measure of character is described here in terms of holiness. *The willingness to continue the relationship shows the positive impact of the Christian spouse's witness on the character of the unbeliever, and so the unbeliever can be said to "be made holy" because of their believing spouse.* And if this is true of the unbelieving wife or husband, how much more will it true of the children within the family (verse 14b), who are even more influenced by the witness of the believing parent? The atmosphere within the home is decisively changed by the impact of the Christian spouse on the unbelieving partner and their children. Calvin, a seasoned pastor himself, commented on this passage that the godliness of the one spouse does more to "sanctify" the marriage than the ungodliness of the other spouse does to make it unclean. But if the unbelieving partner separates, Paul says, let it be so (verse 15a). The believer is henceforth free — they are "not enslaved" (verse 15b). The obvious meaning is that if the unbelieving partner leaves, in spite of the godly witness of the believer, the believing spouse is under no obligation to continue living with the unbeliever. But does he go beyond that to say the believing spouse is therefore free to divorce and presumably remarry? At the end of the chapter he says this: "A wife is bound to her husband as long as he lives" (verse 39). Does this statement govern every situation mentioned in the chapter, including this one? Or does it simply go back to the main theme presented in verse 10 that *Christian* marriages should not be dissolved? In verses 12-16, Paul is addressing a situation pertaining to a minority of cases. He assumes in verse 15a that the unbelieving spouse has already left the home and is not returning. Why would he say that the believing spouse is no longer enslaved to remain with the unbeliever when in fact the unbeliever has already left? Surely he is saying something more. He is acknowledging that the marriage is over and the believer is free to end it formally, and to remarry — though only to another Christian, in light of verse 39b, which states that remarriage must be "in the Lord." Paul was also undoubtedly aware that Jesus made an explicit exception to the rule barring divorce, to the effect that divorce is allowed (though not commanded) in cases of explicit unfaithfulness (Mt. 19:9).

The last statement Paul makes here addresses the believing spouse: how do you know whether you will save your unbelieving spouse once that spouse has left? The statement is open-ended. You might save them or you might not. The point is you don't know. You are not free to give up at the first sign of trouble, because redemption might be just around the corner. Equally, you are not bound to stay within the marriage once the spouse has left simply because there's always a chance they might return and you might lead them to the Lord. They have made their choice, and they are no longer your responsibility. This must be taken alongside Peter's instruction to Christian women married to unbelieving men to live in such a way that by their sacrificial conduct their husbands may be won to Christ (1 Pet. 3:1-6). We are to do everything we can to sustain the marriage, but if it ends through the unbeliever leaving (and probably remarrying), we are free to move on. The believer does not have to spend their life waiting in the false hope that the spouse who has left, and probably remarried, will return. The open-ended nature of the question, however, does call the believing spouse to weigh their actions carefully rather than making rushed decisions.

25 Now concerning the betrothed, I have no command from the Lord, but I give my judgment as one who by the Lord's mercy is trustworthy. 26 I think that in view of the present distress it is good for a person to remain as he is. 27 Are you bound to a wife? Do not seek to be free. Are you free from a wife? Do not seek a wife.

So far in this chapter, Paul has dealt with the issue of freedom in regard to sexual relationships in Christian marriages (verses 1-7), Christians separated or widowed (verses 8-9), people in Christian marriages thinking of separating (verses 10-11), and Christians married to unbelievers (verses 12-16). He has also addressed the issue of freedom in relation to circumcision and slavery (verses 17-24), which we discussed in our previous chapter. In the remainder of chapter 7, he talks about the Christian freedom of those not yet married (verses 25-38), and finishes with a summary statement (verses 39-40).

The word "betrothed" (verse 25) is the Greek word *parthenos*, which refers to a virgin, whether male or female. The ancient sense of the word dealt more with the unmarried condition than the degree of sexual experience. Here, Paul is addressing the situation of people who have never married.

This passage has often been misconstrued to present the idea that Paul was opposed to marriage. In fact, Paul was opposing a party in the Corinthian church who saw marriage as unspiritual, and were advocating the ceasing of sexual relationships even among married couples (verses 1-7). Throughout the chapter, Paul is responding to questions members of the church have sent him as they were facing this kind of teaching.

The key to understanding this passage comes in verse 26. Paul places limits on the freedom of people who have never been married to enter into marriage. But these limits are determined by the meaning of his phrase "in view of the present distress." Historians have discovered evidence that a series of famines hit Greece during the reign of Claudius (AD 41-54), including a particularly severe famine in AD 51. There is localized evidence of the impact on Corinth. The effects of these famines were still reverberating when Paul wrote this letter, probably at the beginning of AD 54. Roman writers spoke of the additional hardships faced by families during such times, and often advised against marriage as a result. Paul uses the word *anagke* (literally "pressure") to refer to this time of distress. He employs the same word in 2 Cor. 12:10 to speak of "hardships" or severe pressures during the course of his ministry. Paul is speaking of a *temporary period of difficulty* the Corinthians were experiencing when he wrote the letter. This is not a general reference to the present age in which we live, even though tribulation and suffering are part and parcel of our experience during this age. What Paul says here must be seen in this light. He is saying something like this: "It is a good course of action to remain unmarried at this present time, given the external circumstances we are facing," *and not* "It is always a good course of action to remain unmarried." This is *not* the same thing as saying the teaching is culturally relative to the first century and true only in those times, but must be reinterpreted today. That is the approach used by liberal theology to deny the present authority of Scripture and then used to place whatever interpretation on the Bible the particular theologian has a liking for. The difference is this. Paul is stating a *universally-valid principle*: in times of severe social distress, it may not be wise to marry and start a family.

Remember that Paul began the chapter by opposing the view of those at Corinth whose statement is quoted in verse 1: "It is good for a man not to have sexual relations with a woman." Against this, he says that in general each man should have his own wife and each woman her own husband (verse 2). However, here he gives an exception to the rule in view of certain temporary social and economic circumstances. In this section, Paul is addressing the "betrothed." These are people not yet married. This issue is clouded by the ESV translation: "Are you bound to a wife? Do not seek to be free. Are you free from a wife? Do not seek a wife." If he is speaking to engaged couples, what does he mean by being bound to a wife? The phrase "do not seek to be free" translates the Greek "do not seek a dissolving of obligations." The "dissolving of obligations" is not a phrase normally used for divorce. Furthermore, the word translated in the ESV as "wife" is actually the Greek word "woman." Here is a more accurate translation of the verse: "Are you betrothed to a woman? Do not seek to end the betrothal. Have you dissolved an engagement? Do not seek a fiancée." But all this is to be seen in light of the phrase "in view of the present distress." Paul is not counseling against marriage, or else he would have counseled to end all engagements from this time forth and forevermore! He is simply advising that if you are not presently engaged, this is not the time to enter into an engagement. And if you have broken off an engagement, it is not the time to re-enter one.

28 But if you do marry, you have not sinned, and if a betrothed woman marries, she has not sinned. Yet those who marry will have worldly troubles, and I would spare you that.

Paul carefully brings balance in verse 28. Especially in times of social and economic hardship, marriage and family life will prove burdensome, yet there is nothing wrong with getting married, a point Paul must make against the ascetic or "super-spiritual" group in Corinth. As a wise pastor, he is giving people the choice while offering his counsel. Christians are free to find their own way in God in the area of marriage, as in other areas of life, but have a responsibility at the same time to listen to godly counsel. Leaders are obligated to give counsel, but must then trust their flock into God's hands for wise decision making.

29 This is what I mean, brothers: the appointed time has grown very short. From now on, let those who have wives live as though they had none, 30 and those who mourn as though they were not mourning, and those who rejoice as though they were not rejoicing, and those who buy as though they had no goods, 31 and those who deal with the world as though they had no dealings with it. For the present form of this world is passing away.

Paul moves on to a further clarification. Greek has two words to express the concept of time. The usual word is *chronos*, which referred to an ordinary duration or period of time. But in verse 29, he uses the word *kairos*. This refers to a specific or special point in time — a critical moment of great significance. The *kairos* has "been shortened" (not "grown very short," as in ESV, which would suggest it was about to end). The meaning is that it has been shortened by a deliberate intervention of God's mercy. This shortened time for Paul means the whole period of the "last days" beginning with Pentecost and ending with the Lord's return. The New Testament consistently identifies the entire church age as the last days (Ac. 2:17-21; Heb. 1:2; Jas. 5:3, 1 Pet. 1:20; 1 Jn. 2:18). During this period, which from God's perspective is short, the whole range of human activities, whether marriage, mourning, rejoicing, buying or selling, must be placed in the perspective of eternity. It is not that these activities are useless or even wrong, it is just that they are not our ultimate purpose in life, and times of particular or extraordinary crisis demonstrate that. And they bring to light our true priorities. Paul is not saying that he believes the return of Christ is imminent. He devotes letters written over many years to a wide range of subjects which assumes Christians have a long life to live. But the present time of crisis and hardship being endured by the Corinthians does remind them (and us) of one great truth: "The present form of this world is passing away" (verse 31). We live in the last days. Christians are to enter into marriage, weep, rejoice and live normal lives, but are to do so in light of eternity.

The last set of phrases is this: "those who deal with the world as though they had no dealings with it." This phrase sheds light on what Paul means by his repeated use in this section of the clause "as though... not." The meaning is that those who buy things are to do so *as though they are not entering into full ownership.* They are to keep a loose hold on their possessions, on their "dealings with the world." Calvin says on this phrase that we are to possess things in such a way that they do not hinder us on our journey. That gives the sense of everything else Paul is saying in these verses. Marriage is not wrong, it is just not the ultimate purpose of our life, which is to live for Christ in light of eternity. All that we do, including marriage, is to be evaluated in light of God's call on our lives. Christians are free, but only to move within the counsel of God's will as the Scriptures, the Holy Spirit and wise counsel reveals it to them. We are to keep our eyes on the journey and on our destination, and allow God to help us see all other things from that perspective.

32 I want you to be free from anxieties. The unmarried man is anxious about the things of the Lord, how to please the Lord. 33 But the married man is anxious about worldly things, how to please his wife, 34 and his interests are divided. And the unmarried or betrothed woman is anxious about the things of the Lord, how to be holy in body and spirit. But the married woman is anxious about worldly things, how to please her husband. 35 I say this for your own benefit, not to lay any restraint upon you, but to promote good order and to secure your undivided devotion to the Lord.

The goal of Paul's counsel throughout this chapter is a proper understanding of freedom. We are not to seek the freedom our present culture teaches us to seek, which is freedom to do what we want. Such freedom is a delusion none of us, even the wealthy and powerful, will achieve. True freedom, he teaches, is found in obeying God's law (Rom. 13:8-10). It is freedom to lay down our rights and to love our neighbor. This is the freedom Paul has sought to model in his own life (1 Cor. 9:1-23). But here, he defines it from yet another perspective — as freedom from anxiety (verse 31). This freedom sounds somewhat self-centered, but not as Paul defines it. The motivational teachers and pagan philosophers influencing the church in Corinth did indeed tackle this topic from a self-centered focus. They taught that the way to inner peace was to ignore the outward circumstances of life, by a kind of mind over matter process, and give way to whatever the unknowable and impersonal forces of Fate decreed. Inner tranquility, they taught, can be achieved by a mystical separation from all that is happening around us. Paul acknowledges the practical reality that the cares of life are a challenge to all of us. But he found the answer instead in Jesus' teaching to seek first the kingdom of God and let him look after the rest (Mt. 6:33). *We can trust our circumstances to God instead of worrying about them, in the confidence that a loving personal God will look after us.* Paul's paraphrase of Jesus' words is found in Phil. 4:11-13: "I have learned in whatever situation I am to be content. I know how to be brought low, and I know how to abound. In any and every circumstance, I have learned the secret of facing plenty and hunger, abundance and need. I can do all things through him who strengthens me."

Paul's freedom is certainly freedom from human anxieties, but that freedom is not a goal in itself. It has a specific purpose. Freedom from human cares enables us to focus our lives instead on pleasing the Lord (verse 32). Freedom *from* is freedom *for!* Paul is concerned for the pastoral well-being of the people to whom he is writing. The present time of crisis in Corinth meant that marriage and family life had become far more burdensome than in normal times. Under such pressures, the married man or woman has divided interests (verse 34a). The phrase means to be pulled in two directions. They carry the burden of each other and of their children. But those who are not married are spared this burden. They are free to devote the energies they have to serving the Lord. Remember that in this latter section of the chapter, Paul is addressing those not yet married. Here he suggests to them that in this present season they may be able to serve the Lord most effectively by remaining single. Paul's point here is pastoral in nature rather than theological. He is not opposed to marriage, as he has made clear throughout the chapter. He is simply advising the unmarried that this time of "present distress" may not be a good moment to make that commitment. His counsel is applicable at any point we are facing times of personal or societal crisis.

36 If anyone thinks that he is not behaving properly toward his betrothed, if his passions are strong, and it has to be, let him do as he wishes: let them marry—it is no sin. 37 But whoever is firmly established in his heart, being under no necessity but having his desire under control, and has determined this in his heart, to keep her as his betrothed, he will do well. 38 So then he who marries his betrothed does well, and he who refrains from marriage will do even better.

Paul addresses the men who are engaged: if the strain is so great to the point a young man is continually tempted to act in a sexually inappropriate manner, he and his betrothed should marry, for it is no sin. The phrase "his passions are too strong" translates the Greek word *huperakmos*, which means literally something beyond the limits. The man has reached the limits of restraint and so should marry. Paul is not interested in promoting the asceticism the Corinthians were advocating. He is not opposed to marriage, and he advocates a healthy sexual relationship within marriage. His concern is for the well-being of young believers facing a period of great distress. If they are able to live without marrying, then — at least for a season — let them do so. If not, they should go ahead and marry, to avoid falling into sexual sin.The decision to delay marriage must be reached out of a sense of firm spiritual conviction — he is "firmly established in his heart, being under no necessity" (verse 37a). "Necessity" is the Greek word *anagke,* the same word used in verse 26 to describe the time of present pressure in society. Young believers are pulled between the pressure of external social circumstances and the pressure of their love for one another. It's important to note that for Paul in the end the pressure of love takes precedence over the pressures life is throwing against us. It's only if they feel under no pressure to marry that they should refrain or delay. Once all these factors are considered, the young couple are free to "do as they wish" (verse 36). In the final analysis, believers must come to their own conclusions. If they are wise, they will take pastoral advice, but they are in the end responsible for their own lives and, of course, must then take the consequences of their actions. A wise pastor or parents will give their counsel, and then stand back and trust God with what happens.

39 A wife is bound to her husband as long as he lives. But if her husband dies, she is free to be married to whom she wishes, only in the Lord. 40 Yet in my judgment she is happier if she remains as she is. And I think that I too have the Spirit of God.

We now arrive at the chapter's conclusion. Paul starts by making the point that remarriage can only be to a fellow Christian (verse 39). Believers are never free to marry unbelievers. For a Christian to marry a non-Christian is unthinkable. The apostle's last words of counsel are that a widow may be happier if she stays as she is (verse 40). His assertion that he also has the Spirit of God does not mean he is claiming some kind of infallible authority. It is meant simply to counteract the ascetic group at Corinth who almost certainly claimed to be speaking with the authority of the Spirit. This was only part of the general disorder in the church, much of it caused by people claiming to possess the Spirit in special measure, while in fact acting in an immature or even ungodly manner. Paul does not claim to possess an authority which overrides the freedom of believers to do as they wish, so long as it is in obedience to the Lord. His authority is given by God to upbuild the body (2 Cor. 10:8), but that is the very reason his counsel should be listened to, not only by the Corinthians, but by us who read his words today.

ELEVEN

FREEDOM, WIVES AND HUSBANDS

Ephesians 5 contains perhaps the most profound teaching on marriage in the New Testament. It also contains a powerful message on the nature of Christian freedom.

18 And do not get drunk with wine, for that is debauchery, but be filled with the Spirit.

The stage is set in verse 18, where Paul offers us this command: "Be filled with the Spirit." The only way husbands or wives will be able to fulfill the call to married life about to be described is by the empowering of the Spirit. Our own best efforts will not cut it. There are two significant things about Paul's phrase. One is the *present tense*, which means "Be repeatedly filled." The Holy Spirit is always available to help us, but we have to ask, and do so regularly. The other is that the command is *in the plural*. He's speaking to the entire church to which he's writing. The command is corporate. It's for all of us together. God wants a Spirit-filled church, not just a few

Spirit-filled individuals.

21 submitting to one another out of reverence for Christ.

Just a few words later comes a direct application of this phrase: we are to submit to one another. A people filled with the Spirit are a submitted people, a people ready to follow Jesus in the way of the cross. This command applies to every believer without exception. The word "submit" *(hupotassomenoi)* is a Greek middle participle. The word means to choose voluntarily to place oneself under a structure or order, an order which, in this case, God himself has created. Each of us chooses to place ourselves under this order for the greater good of the whole, thus sacrificing a measure of our own personal freedom to do what we want. God has the right to command, but here, through Paul, he chooses to appeal. Why? Because he wants a submission that comes from our choice, something that springs up from within our heart. The submission is first of all to him, but also to one another. We live in an upside-down kingdom where the king became the servant of all, and teaches us to follow his example. We are all in humility to count others "more significant" than ourselves (Phil. 2:3). *The body of Christ is a submitted place.* It's not a place for lone rangers or people looking out for themselves. But such restriction of our personal freedom can only come out of a life that is being continually re-filled with the Spirit. You can't do it on your own strength. By nature, we are far more invested in our own interests than in anyone else's. We love our independence!

Immediately following this appeal, Paul launches into what Biblical scholars call a "household code" — instructions for how Christians are to conduct themselves in their relationships with each other. He begins with husbands and wives, continues with parents and children, and moves finally to slaves and masters (in our terms, employees and employers). It quickly becomes clear that this code of conduct puts limits on the freedom of each and every believer. *Freedom is not the liberty to do what we want. It is the liberty to do what God wants.* Yet this mutual submission is exactly where true freedom is found. Writing to the Corinthians, Paul says boldly that "where the Spirit of the Lord is, there is freedom" (2 Cor. 3:17). Here he writes to the Ephesians, urging them to seek daily the filling of the same Spirit, and showing them the true freedom the Spirit will lead them into. Without prejudging the place of spiritual gifts today, we can say that the freedom Paul talks about both in 2 Corinthians and here deals not with charismatic experiences, but with the wider subject of leading a Christ-like life. We are free to lay our lives down for Christ and for one another, but only the Spirit can enable us to do it.

The household code of conduct that Paul unfolds appears in fairly similar form in other places (Col. 3:18-4:1; 1 Pet. 2:18-3:7; 1 Tim. 2:8-15; 6:1-10; Tit. 2:1-10), so it is not just an afterthought. The Greek world also had its lists of how relationships in society should operate. But there are substantial differences to what Paul says. For the Greeks, including Plato and Aristotle, women and slaves were regarded as inferior in all respects, but Paul addresses them as of equal worth and value: "In Christ there is neither slave nor free, there is no male and female, for you are all one in Christ Jesus" (Gal. 3:28). In Paul's household instructions, women are asked to make a free choice to submit to an order which gives the husband a greater measure of responsibility to look after his family. That is radically different from the pagan culture in which women, like slaves, were an afterthought whose opinion and choice didn't matter. His view of the husband's role of leadership is likewise very different from the unlimited power the man held in the pagan view of marriage. The Christian husband, by contrast, turns out to be first and foremost a servant. Paul's view of slaves and slavery was also profoundly counter-cultural, as we outlined in chapter nine. He had a valued relationship with the runaway slave Onesimus. Paul appealed to Philemon, Onesimus' master, to entertain a radical change of attitude toward his slave. He urged people not to go along with the pagan practice of selling themselves into slavery for financial gain: don't become "slaves of men" (1 Cor. 7:23).

The model for the pattern of mutual submission about to unfold is always Christ who, being God, humbled himself and took on the form of a slave. The goal of submission is always ultimately to please Christ. *Thus Paul relativizes and alters the absolute authority structures of marriage and slavery dominating the culture in which he lived.* The purpose of similar sets of instructions in the Roman world was to keep the lower classes in their place and reinforce the privilege of the rulers, be they husbands or slave-owners. Husbands held the power of life and death over their wives and children. They kept that authority even when their children married, and could even initiate divorce proceedings on behalf of their daughter if they wanted to (and regardless of the daughter's wishes). Jewish households, especially in the Diaspora (Jewish communities outside of Palestine) were somewhat similar. The purpose of Paul's instructions is very different. His goal is not to repress anyone or give anyone unfair advantage, but rather to provide a demonstration to pagan culture how a Spirit-empowered people relate in love and service to one another.

Our study will quickly lead us into territory as controversial in our modern pagan culture as Paul's words were in the pagan culture of his day (though for different reasons, which reminds us Biblical truth consistently offends pagan culture, no matter where that culture is coming from). And we are called to receive his words as the expression of God's heart and law for us, part of the body of Scripture that, as Jesus made clear, cannot be broken (Jn. 10:35). But we need to be very careful to understand what he is and isn't saying.

22 Wives, submit to your own husbands, as to the Lord. 23 For the husband is the head of the wife even as Christ is the head of the church, his body, and is himself its Savior. 24 Now as the church submits to Christ, so also wives should submit in everything to their husbands.

Within the context of being filled with the Spirit, and submitting mutually one to another, and understanding Paul's fundamental theological point that men and women are equal in worth and value, he now urges wives to submit to their husbands. Again, as in verse 21, the verb is in the middle aspect. There, his address was to everyone, but here it is specifically directed to the married women. He appeals to the wives to make a voluntary decision to submit to an order God has established in marriage for the common good. It is important to note he is not telling women to be subject to men in general, in which case he would have used different words. Wives are to submit to their own husbands only. The submission of the wife is shaped by a very important phrase, "as to the Lord." Her submission to her husband is an expression of her decision to submit to Christ. Her submission to Christ is the cornerstone and foundation of her submission to her husband. She does not submit to her husband because he carries greater worth or standing in the world, as the Romans, Greeks and many of the Jews believed, but because she is submitted to Christ. This restriction of her outward freedom is what Christ has asked her to do as part of the order he has created, which is to benefit everyone without exception and without bias.

The reason for this submission is given in the next verse: "For the husband is the head of the wife even as Christ is the head of the church" (verse 23). The context of Paul's theology, as he sets it forth here, indicates quite clearly he has lines of authority in mind. Christ is head over everything, and everything has been placed under his feet (Eph. 1:22). The lines of authority Paul is laying out, however, have nothing to do with a person's worth or value. They are functional in nature. All believers are to carry a submissive attitude evidenced by a willingness to serve each other, but wives are to respect the place of government or leadership God has given their husbands in the home. This is a restriction on the wife's freedom, but in due course we will find out that the husband's freedom is restricted also, and perhaps even more fundamentally. Paul's appeal to the wife, within the context of the passage as a whole, is a challenge to pagan culture in several highly significant ways. First, her submission is voluntary, grounded in her submission to Christ. Second, whereas Roman law in Paul's day placed the woman under her father's authority even after married, Paul insists that the husband, not the father-in-law, is the head of the home. Third, the husband's authority is restricted to actions which truly benefit the wife. Fourth, no human authority is given ultimate power. The wife is called to submit to her husband, but the entire church, husbands included, must submit to Christ (verse 24). To respect her husband's authority does not mean Paul would require the wife to do anything contrary to God's law, any more than he would counsel Christian citizens to obey laws that force them to disobey God. Nonetheless, the wife is called to a stance of faith that, if she allows the husband to take ultimate responsibility for decisions into which she has had her input, the Lord will honor her step of faith by turning those decisions for her good and the good of the family.

25 Husbands, love your wives, as Christ loved the church and gave himself up for her, 26 that he might sanctify her, having cleansed her by the washing of water with the word, 27 so that he might present the church to himself in splendor, without spot or wrinkle or any such thing, that she might be holy and without blemish. 28 In the same way husbands should love their wives as their own bodies. He who loves his wife loves himself.

Next the husbands are addressed, and at far greater length. They are commanded to love their wives (verse 25). The command is in the present tense, which emphasizes ongoing action. This is a love that carries on through thick and thin. The verb is *agapao,* a word rarely used in secular Greek, and which emphasizes unconditional love regardless of merit. It is the verb the New Testament particularly adopts to describe the love of

Christ for his people. Nowhere in the New Testament is this Greek word used to call wives to love their husbands. It is particularly the husband's responsibility to walk in this way, reflecting the sacrificial, self-giving love of Christ for the church.

Nowhere in Jewish, Greek or Roman literature, or even in the Old Testament, is such an exhortation to husbands found. It is unique. And it is radical, for it calls the husband to lay down his life unconditionally, regardless of his wife's response. The husband's role of leadership in the home is to be expressed in the same way Christ expressed his leadership — by giving up everything he had for those he led. To understand the husband's position as either a tyrant whose every whim is to be obeyed, or a self-centered narcissist whose every need is to be served, is to misunderstand entirely the nature of Christian marriage. God has given the husband an authority even as he gave Christ authority, but his leadership is to be exercised in the best interests of his wife and children. The husband is to nurture his wife so that he may present her to Christ in the same condition Christ presents the church to the Father — without stain or wrinkle (verses 26-27). He is to do all he can to cause her relationship with Christ to flourish, and if that happens she will surely find the purposes for which God created her to be fulfilled. She will become everything God designed her to be. They are to love their wives as they love themselves (verse 28). It is natural for them to look after themselves, and it should be just as natural for them to look after their wives. And they are to do so in the same unconditional way Christ loved the church. It is part of the husband's obedience to the Lord. And it brings true freedom to husband and wife alike.

29 For no one ever hated his own flesh, but nourishes and cherishes it, just as Christ does the church, 30 because we are members of his body. 31 "Therefore a man shall leave his father and mother and hold fast to his wife, and the two shall become one flesh."

This is further amplified in verse 29, where Paul talks about the husband "nourishing" and "cherishing" his wife. This love is compared to Christ's love for the church. The husband must walk in the self-sacrificial steps of Christ. By this comparison, husbands are set a standard impossible to meet, except by the help of the Holy Spirit. This draws us back to the idea of the constant need for the filling of the Spirit (verse 18). This continual filling is the basis God provides for us to live in community, each restricting their own freedom for the good of others. And for no group is this more true than the husbands.

We are all pictured here as part of Christ's body. The church is an organism, not an organization, a family not a firm. Churches are intended to be communities, not corporations. The idea Paul expresses of being part of Christ's body in the context of a discussion on marriage draws him back to Genesis: "Therefore a man shall leave his father and mother and hold fast to his wife, and the two shall become one flesh" (verse 31). In verse 28, he commanded husbands to love their wives as their own bodies. Now he draws from the account of the very first marriage the thought that husband and wife are in some mysterious way one flesh. The verb "hold fast" means literally to be "glued together." The idea is not that their individual natures no longer exist, but that each person is enlarged and enriched through their union with the other. Marriage in Christ brings about a transformation which unalterably changes both partners, and causes each to dedicate themselves to the good of the other. The restriction in freedom this entails for both husband and wife is more than compensated for by the gift each partner is to the other. And thus a greater and truer freedom results, the freedom to be one flesh in Christ and to serve him together.

32 This mystery is profound, and I am saying that it refers to Christ and the church.

The idea of union is indeed a mystery. The word "mystery" in the New

Testament refers to something hidden but now revealed by God. Paul uses it earlier in Ephesians to talk of the mystery of the joining together of Jews and Gentiles in Christ (Eph. 3:3-6). Paul's subject in these verses is that conduct in marriage is to be based on the conduct of Christ toward the church (verses 28-30). He then quotes Genesis regarding the union of man and woman in marriage (verse 31). This leads him finally to say that the real mystery being revealed is not just the union of man and woman in marriage, but even more so the greater union of Christ and the church. Marriage never gains meaning more than when we realize it is intended to be the closest human reflection of the love of Christ for his church.

33 However, let each one of you love his wife as himself, and let the wife see that she respects her husband.

Paul brings the section to a conclusion. This is not a command for the husband to love himself first, then love his wife in the same way. Self-love is a characteristic of fallen humanity, and in general needs little encouragement. The husband is to love his wife because they are one flesh. The addition of the word "each" in Greek adds the emphasis that no husband is excluded from the command. This is *agape* love, the unconditional self-sacrificial love of Christ, the love that took Christ to the cross. It is, as we said before, a standard reachable only by the daily empowering of the Spirit.

There is a significant contrast when it comes to the wife's response. For the husband, the direction comes in the form of a Greek command: "Let him love his wife as himself." But for the wife, there is an unusual phrase, not a command, translated in the ESV as "let the wife see that she respects her husband." The Greek wording stresses the freedom of decision given to the woman. It has the same general meaning as the phrase, "Wives, submit to your husbands" (verse 22). The idea in both statements is that the wife makes a voluntary decision to place herself in God's order under her husband's authority. We could paraphrase the wording in this way: "I appeal to the wife to make a free choice to respect her husband." The husband is commanded, but the wife is appealed to.

The reasons for the difference are tied up with the Biblical concept of freedom. The husband represents Christ, the bridegroom, and the wife represents the church as the bride. Even as Christ followed the Father in obedience, so the husband must do the same in laying down his life for his wife. *He is given a place of freedom, but only as the one to whom responsibility has been given.* This freedom is dangerous if not properly exercised, and it must be defined very carefully so that its exercise benefits those are led. Hence the command given to the husband. There is no hint of free choice. It's an order. But it is different when we come to the wife. Even as the church, composed of its individual members, makes the decision freely to submit to Christ as Savior, so the wife is urged to make the free decision to submit to her husband.

What is the point Paul is trying to make? The holding of authority, even in the hands of redeemed but imperfect humanity, can always lead to abuse. Submitting to human authority, therefore, always involves risk. That is why the demands on the husband must be greater than those on the wife. That is why his freedom must be limited so that his actions only bring benefit to his wife. And that is also why the wife submits to the husband *only insofar as he is the representative of Christ.* She is not forced into a fallen social order in which the men hold dictatorial authority and are often abusive. That was the social situation into which Paul was writing, and sadly, it is all too often the case today. In Gen. 3:16, we find these words: "Your desire shall be contrary to your husband, but he shall rule over you." They express the consequences of the fall for the marriage relationship. The Hebrew verb "rule" suggests that Adam holds an authority that is abusive, while the Hebrew verb "desire" pictures Eve as seeking control through manipulation, presumably for her own protection. The result is conflict, a battle between abuse on the one hand, and self-protection through control on the other. Most of us, sadly, know couples whose relationship follows this dynamic. The solution is found in the lifting of the curse in Christ, and this has a direct application to redeeming fallen marriages. That is what this passage is all about. The husband's freedom to rule abusively is curtailed, so that his actions must now benefit his wife. The wife's freedom to live in independence or manipulative control of her husband is also restricted, so that she makes the decision to trust that the God who gave her husband the responsibility to rule will hold him to account if he does not exercise that responsibility properly. Relationships which do not take these admonitions seriously may seem to offer a false freedom and independence, but will over time tend to fall back into the default mode of abuse and control as pictured in Genesis.

Many Christian couples could share their own perspective on what this looks like in practice. An important part of it is that no important decisions are taken without mutual agreement. This is a restriction on the freedom of both husband and wife. The husband's headship is best described as the one who in the end has to take responsibility for the decision made. In the process, a wise husband will make sure his wife is fully informed and has herself freely owned the decision. The husband also carries a role of spiritual and physical protection. Any husband should be ready to protect his wife from physical attack, but the same truth applies in the spiritual realm. He should never leave her alone to face the serpent, as Adam did with Eve. The husband should always be ready to go to war in prayer on behalf of his wife. He should be sensitive when she feels under attack or being criticized by others. The husband also carries a responsibility for what goes on in the home. His role does not end at his place of employment, after which he comes home and selfishly expects to be waited on. He is ultimately responsible before God for his wife and children, and that responsibility extends to co-laboring with his wife in running the household. How that works out will differ from couple to couple, but the important principle is that it is worked out by mutual agreement. Husbands and wives are not meant to be ships passing in the night. They are each other's best friends and closest companions. Each of us gains by the contribution the other brings. My wife has had such profound influence on me that even when you hear me preaching or teaching, or when you read these words, you are hearing her, sometimes even more than me, even if you aren't aware of it.

The road to a Biblically-based marriage is not easy, but it is a road worth traveling. It is a road to freedom. The alternative is two people leading their own independent but intersecting lives. Some people profess to find happiness that way. Many more don't. Co-dependency is no match for both parties being dependent on God. Dysfunctional marriages have been compared to two people who bring drinks with straws to the table and proceed to sip as fast as they can out of their partner's cup. When they have drunk each other dry, the marriage is over.

How much better to follow God's way! He has an infinite supply of the water of life. Instead of sticking your straw into someone else's cup, try sticking it into his. It's a well that will never run dry. When both partners get that straight, they will have a successful marriage. Many people try sincerely to love their spouse as best they can. But how foolish it is not to go to that well that never runs out. Freedom to act either by abuse or through control is not an option that will save any marriage. Giving up your freedom and asking for God's help will. And in the end you'll find a freedom far greater and deeper than anything your own stubborn independence will give you.

TWELVE

FREEDOM, PARENTS AND CHILDREN

1 Children, obey your parents in the Lord, for this is right. 2 "Honor your father and mother" (this is the first commandment with a promise), 3 "that it may go well with you and that you may live long in the land." (Eph 6:1-3)

Just as in the previous section, two parties are addressed, and limits are placed on the freedom of each. The phrase "in the Lord" does not refer to the fact that the parents are Christians, but points to the nature of the children's obedience. It is "in the Lord," which means it is part of their Christian responsibility, regardless of whether the parents are believers or not. The fact that children are not free to exercise unlimited freedom is a common-sense reality, yet the specific restriction of their freedom in placing them under the authority of their mother and father is increasingly less respected in the postmodern culture in which we live.

It's interesting that Paul addresses children as having enough grasp of spiritual truth that they are capable of instruction. Churches should call children up, not dumb them down! Youth groups should be full of Biblical teaching and discipleship training, not just fun and games. Paul goes on to quote the fifth commandment from the Greek Old Testament of Exod. 21:12 and Deut. 5:16. This is the first commandment with a specific promise attached to it (the second commandment has a more general promise). This shows once again that Paul considered the law in its moral dimension to be as applicable today as it was then. Honor is equated with obedience, and is to be given to both parents, not just the father, who is the Biblical head of the family. The mother is to be treated with equal honor, which correlates with the honor and care with which her husband is to treat her.

The call to obedience means that the freedom of the children is restricted. As children get older, their desire for a freedom which may prove harmful for them deepens, and so they must be instructed and trained to avoid such dangers. In return for this obedience, children will be given the Old Testament promise of a long life on the earth (verse 3). This is because they have learned to structure their lives in obedience to God and his will, thus saving them untold harm in following the ways of this world. Under the old covenant, the promise of long life in the land was given on condition of the keeping of the law (Deut. 5:33). Christians are still called to keep the law, not as in the old sacrificial system, but in its moral aspect as fulfilled in Christ (Mt. 5:17; Rom. 8:4; 13:8-10). This long life is not lived out in the land of Israel, as under the old covenant, but wherever in the earth believers are found. This is in line with the fact that the church, composed of Jews and Gentiles, has inherited the Old Testament promises of the land and are able to take spiritual possession not only of the land of Israel, as under the old covenant, but are commissioned to extend the boundaries of the kingdom throughout the whole earth (Mt. 24:14; 28:19).

4 Fathers, do not provoke your children to anger, but bring them up in the discipline and instruction of the Lord.

Next Paul turns to the fathers. The mothers deserve equal obedience and honor, but the fathers carry the ultimate responsibility of headship. And the fathers in particular need to be addressed, because the role of the father in pagan culture was frequently carried out in a way displeasing to God. Under Roman law, the father had more power over a son than a master had over a slave. He could imprison him, sell him into slavery or even have him executed. In the Judaism of the Roman Empire children, like slaves, were considered inferior. Fathers were as gods to them.

Paul's words must have come as a shock to many fathers: "Fathers, do not provoke your children to anger." Instead of reinforcing their almost unlimited freedom to act as they wanted toward their children, Paul begins by placing a serious restriction on it. The command is in the present tense, emphasizing it is a continuous responsibility. Fathers are to be less concerned with punishing their children's attitudes than with preventing those attitudes from forming in the first place.

Fathers are called not to provoke their children, but on the other hand (the little word "but" in Greek carries some force) they are to discipline and instruct them, and they are to do so in the context of their own obedience to the Lord. No longer is the father a god in his house. It is not the father's will, but God's will, which is to be done. "Discipline" refers not to beating them, but to teaching them. "Training" would be a good equivalent. "Instruction" conveys the idea of appeal or gentle admonition, not roughly ordering them about.

Paul paints a picture radically different from the pagan society in which the first Christians lived. Instead of having freedom to do what they want, ruling with an iron fist and without any concern for the well being of anyone other than themselves, fathers must come under the order of authority in which God has placed them. Their authority is merely delegated. God determines the boundaries of that authority, as well as the proper goals of its exercise. *The exercise of a father's authority is to be for the benefit of his children, not for the benefit of himself.* So we find that the father's freedom toward his children is greatly restricted by comparison with the standards of the prevailing culture, and this is in direct parallel with the restrictions on the freedom of the husband in his conduct toward his wife. Even though the two relationships are different, one fundamental truth is the same: husbands and fathers are to exercise their leadership by serving both their wives and their children.

THIRTEEN

FREEDOM IN
THE CHURCH

One of the most justifiable critiques of church life in our western culture deals with its weak understanding of Biblical church government. Churches are often built on ideas drawn from the corporate world, which have little resemblance to the Biblical model. And then we wonder why they do not operate effectively.

It turns out this has a lot to do with how we understand freedom. Much church government is a trade-off between church members and pastors, in which both parties seek to preserve aspects of their own freedom rather than each laying it down in the greater interests of the kingdom. This has disastrous results, and the church frequently winds up looking more like a poorly-run corporation than a Biblical family.

To understand how Christian freedom is meant to operate in the context of church life requires us to lay a brief foundation of the New Testament understanding of church government and the responsibilities of church members (a much longer treatment of this subject is available in my book *Landmarks: A Comprehensive Look at the Foundations of Faith)*. This in turn should lead us into a deeper understanding of how freedom and personal independence operate within the setting of the local church.

THE BIBLICAL BASIS OF ELDERSHIP

The basic format of New Testament church government is expressed in the office of eldership. When the apostles established elders in every congregation, as Paul did from the beginning (Ac. 14:23) to the end (Tit. 1:5) of his ministry, they were not inventing a new practice. They were primarily influenced by the existence of the office of eldership within the covenant people of God since ancient times. The Hebrew word for elder (*zaqen*) can refer simply to an older man, but more often it refers to one chosen by God to give leadership among his people. The presence of elders is found from the days of Moses. When God appeared to Moses in the desert, he was commanded to return to Egypt and gather together the elders of Israel (Exod. 3:16), who represented the spiritual leadership of the people of Israel under Egyptian rule. At God's command, Moses appointed a specific body of elders to represent God to the people (Num. 11:16-30). This seems to lay a foundation for the selection of elders; they are appointed by existing spiritual leadership, not elected by the people. As such, they represent God to the people, not the people to God. Throughout the Old Testament, elders appear in three forms, the elders of Israel or the nation as a whole (Exod. 3:18; 1 Sam. 4:3; 2 Chron. 5:14; Ezek. 14:1); the elders of cities or towns (Deut. 19:12; Judg. 8:14; 2 Kgs. 10:1) and elders who served the king (2 Sam.12:17; 1 Kgs. 12:6). In these various settings, elders offered spiritual counsel, as well as handling governmental leadership and the administration of justice. They advised the leaders of the nation, whether Moses, Joshua or the various kings. They governed the affairs of each town and administered justice. There is no indication that elders were appointed by any other means than the community (or more likely, the existing body of elders) recognizing the hand of God upon them. There is no record of any occasion where God allowed the people to choose whomever they wanted.

Elders continued to govern Israel under Greek and Roman rule. The Sanhedrin was the national council of elders, while local elders governed each synagogue. So from before the days of Moses until after the time of Jesus, and while other forms of government (judges, prophets, kings and foreign rulers) came and went, elders remained as a basic expression of leadership among the Jewish people. It is no surprise that at a very early stage the church adopted the same form of government. The apostles in the Jerusalem church had begun to transition their leadership to an eldership as early as the Jerusalem council in Acts 15.

This also explains why eldership always appears as a plurality in the early church, for elders in the Old Testament always appear as a group. The New Testament does have other words for local church leadership, for instance, overseer, leader, shepherd and helmsman. These are probably best understood not as offices distinct from eldership, but as words describing the function of elders. See Paul's address to the *elders* at Ephesus: "Pay careful attention to yourselves and to all the flock, in which the Holy Spirit has made you *overseers*, to care for [lit: *shepherd*] the church of God, which he obtained with his own blood" (Ac. 20:27-28). Paul equates elders and overseers in other places (compare 1 Tim. 3:1 and 5:17; Tit. 1:6-7), as does Peter (1 Pet. 5:1-2).

Apostles like Paul appointed elders for every congregation they established (Ac. 14:23). This they did at the direction of the Holy Spirit. There is no mention of an eldership election being held! It is a Biblical principle, established since the days of Moses, that leadership is appointed by God to represent his desires to the people. Leadership serves at God's pleasure, and until removed by God. Unfortunately, the church in our western culture has adopted practices which may work well in civil society, but do not function ideally in church government. Elders in our church culture are often elected to represent the people to God, thus turning on its head the order God established. Elders are frequently elected to serve brief terms and are then replaced by others. There is little concept of elders as spiritual fathers (or mothers, in churches where women also hold the office), people who are committed to serve for the long term. They hold their authority at the discretion of the members of the congregation. They are often chosen because no one else can be found to sit on a corporate-style board. Such a view of Biblical leadership would have been unheard of in the New Testament church.

To re-establish Biblical foundations is not easy, but an increasingly large number of churches are doing so, usually by allowing a godly senior leader to appoint individuals from within the congregation, often with the help of respected outside counsel. Once eldership is established, it becomes self-perpetuating. The existing elders seek their own younger successors. A wise leadership will present proposed names to the congregation to allow for any objections on Biblical grounds. Elders then serve for as long as they feel they can, subject to their continuing to reflect the standards of Biblical conduct set out in the relevant New Testament passages. Financial affairs of the church are conducted by deacons, allowing for separation of spiritual and administrative functions according to the principle set out in Acts 6, where the apostles did not want to neglect their basic mission and become entangled in financial matters.

Only God can truly create an elder. All the church does is recognize the gift God has put in place. If someone is truly an elder, their gift will be acknowledged long before they receive a formal appointment. When a name of a prospective elder is announced, there should be a collective "Amen" from the congregation. If there isn't, trouble is brewing. You cannot impose elders on a congregation which cannot receive them as such. So the process of eldership appointment is neither dictatorship nor democracy. It is relationally-based Biblical Christianity in action!

All this establishes one foundational truth. Elders carry government vested in them by the Holy Spirit. It is not an option for either them or those they care for to treat the church as a democratic institution composed of autonomous individuals, in which everyone contributes a token amount to the common mission while fundamentally retaining their own personal identity and independence. Where this happens, the church often becomes little more than a religious version of the Rotary Club. The kingdom of God brings with it the government of God, as expressed in the local eldership. This concept of spiritual authority challenges our understanding of the church as little more than a collection of individuals attending religious services. It mobilizes us into a divinely-empowered army on a mission. Why this does not degenerate into an ungodly authoritarianism becomes clear as we look at the limits God places on the freedom of elders. Elders in fact wind up with less freedom than those they govern.

Let's look at several New Testament passages which address the interaction between elders and people. We find that freedom is an important theme, even when it is not explicitly mentioned. As in other areas of relationship, freedom in personal conduct, far from being seen as a desirable goal, is subordinated to the requirements of God's kingdom. This applies across the board. For the kingdom to work, everyone must sacrifice aspects of their personal freedom.

12 We ask you, brothers, to respect those who labor among you and are over [lit. "rule"] you in the Lord and admonish you, 13 and to esteem them very highly in love because of their work. Be at peace among yourselves.

(1 Thess. 5:12-13)

Significantly, when addressing the people, Paul begins not with a command but an appeal. This is the first sign that church leaders cannot operate in unrestricted freedom. Their authority is not to be exercised for its own sake, but for the sake of those under their care. But very quickly it becomes apparent that the freedom of church members is likewise restricted. They are called upon to respect their leaders. The functions of the leaders are described three ways. First, they *labor among* the people — whether through teaching, discipleship, pastoral care or supporting the poor, all of which appear in Paul's letters as leadership responsibilities. Second, they *rule over* them. This is a strong word used sometimes of Roman officials, though it is qualified by the phrase "in the Lord," meaning their authority comes from the Lord, not themselves. It is a delegated authority given for God's purposes, not those of the leaders. And it is a rulership that expresses care, for Paul says a man must be able to "rule over" (same word) his own household in order to "care for" the church (1 Tim. 3:5). Thirdly, they admonish those in their care. This word has a note of discipline in it, and is used in verse 14 in connecting with admonishing the idle. But Paul makes it clear elsewhere that even admonishing is done with a view of the welfare of those being addressed: "Do not look on him as an enemy, but admonish him as a brother" (2 Thess. 3:15).

The church members are not only to respect their leaders, but to esteem them very highly. The adverb "very highly" is emphatic. This signifies far more than just a grumbling or passive acceptance. It is an enthusiastic endorsement. And they are to do so "in love." Earlier in the letter, Paul described his own love exercised toward the congregation. He cared for them "like a nursing mother" (2:7), and exhorted and encouraged them "like a father" (2:11). Now he calls for the same love to be exercised by the people toward the leaders. He concludes by urging them to be at peace with one another. Peace is a state of health and the opposite of ferment and unrest. Part of a leader's job is to admonish, and those admonished should respond in peace and submission, not anger and rebellion. A church at peace with itself and with its leaders is a healthy church.

From this short description of church life, it becomes apparent that a proper understanding of freedom is essential to the functioning of a healthy church. The church is part of an upside-down kingdom. The primary purpose of leaders is to serve, and to do so in love. This keeps the church safe from any kind of wrong authoritarianism or abusive leadership. On the other hand, church members are called to a genuine submission. The church is not a democracy; it is an expression of God's kingdom rule. Church members must allow leaders to speak into their lives, or they cannot do their job. Ultimately, it is a person's responsibility to make their own decisions, but they should do so after having given the greatest consideration to the counsel given them. Churches in western culture often operate on principles derived from the world, not the Bible. Leaders exercise authority with a view to strengthening their own position, and members resist any intrusions on the right to conduct their life the way they want to. This sets up the same abuse/control pattern which we saw goes back to Adam and Eve. It leads predictably to strong independent leaders, strong independent church members, lots of strife between them — and weak and unhealthy churches.

7 Remember your leaders, those who spoke to you the word of God. Consider the outcome of their way of life, and imitate their faith.... 17 Obey your leaders and submit to them, for they are keeping watch over your souls, as those who will have to give an account. Let them do this with joy and not with groaning, for that would be of no advantage to you. (Heb. 13:7, 17)

These verses from the writer of Hebrews present another clear indication that church members are not free to conduct their lives as they want. Their freedom is restricted in the greater interest of a healthy church. The context of this instruction is the attempt by some people to introduce what the writer calls "strange teachings" into the church (see verse 9). This seems to represent returning to a form of Judaism, in all probability to escape more of the persecution the church has already experienced in the past (10:34). In many parts of the Roman Empire, Jews were exempt from the requirement to worship the emperor, whereas Christians were not.

The community is first admonished to remember the foundations their leaders laid in their teaching of Scripture and sound doctrine, reinforced by the personal example of their lives and faith (verse 7). The implication is that the authority of leaders is a gift from God which is authenticated by their godly lives and their accurate and Spirit-anointed preaching of the Word. We generally understand that a leader must be of godly character, but we tend to put too little emphasis on the fact they must also be able to teach their flock and to do it well. A leader may operate in a charismatic gift or have a powerful platform personality, but without an ability to teach the Scriptures clearly and powerfully, their authority will tend to be rooted more in their own personality than in the anointing of the Spirit. And the church may wind up a mile wide and an inch deep. Leaders are not put in place simply by human appointment or ecclesiastical process, but by a divine commissioning, which is evident in the fruit of their lives and their authority in the Word. The integrity of Christian leadership cannot be divorced from the evidence of Spirit-anointed faithful, accurate and life-changing exposition of the Scriptures. A ministry that derives from anything less, whether that be popularity, platform presence or political manoeuvring, will do little to extend the boundaries of God's kingdom.

In verses 10-16, the writer goes on to give the antidote to the false teaching which has been circulating. He gives some foundational teaching about the sacrifice of Christ and the end of the Old Testament sacrificial system the false teachers are trying to lure the congregation back into. But the key to resisting the false teachers is to obey the leaders God has placed over them (verse 17a). The word translated "obey" is *peithesthai,* which refers to a persuasion or conviction the person has had to surrender their independence. This persuasion can only come from the Holy Spirit. People who respect church leadership simply because they've been told to, but have no conviction about it, will back out as soon as their own independence or immaturity is challenged. But church members who are mature are willing to submit to those God has appointed as their leaders.

The reason given for the submission of the church members is that their leaders are watching over their souls as those who must give account (verse 17bc). The picture is partly drawn from the common Biblical theme of the shepherd watching his sheep, and partly from Ezekiel's vision of the watchmen who must warn the people of their disobedience and who will be judged if they fail in their duty (Ezek. 33:1-11). Leaders are answerable to God for their oversight. This means that the freedom of leaders to conduct themselves is, if anything, *more restricted than the freedom of those under their care.* The Roman centurion (Mt. 8:5-13) understood that his authority was merely delegated. This is because in the Roman world, Caesar was the only one who held authority in himself. All other authority was delegated. This understanding enabled the centurion to perceive that Jesus was operating under an authority delegated to him that could only have come from one place. This in turn gave the centurion boundless confidence in Jesus' authority and released faith that healed his servant. Scripture says Jesus was astonished at his insight — and it must have taken a lot for Jesus to be astonished! The same idea is in view here. Leaders have an authority which is not theirs. It has been given to them, and they themselves are under a greater authority. God calls them to account for how they have handled it. Put another way, *you can only exercise as much authority as you are submitted to.* This is one reason why in the New Testament leaders or elders always appear in the plural. Even within leadership there should be a mutual accountability. In New Testament days, apostolic ministry also held elders to account, and churches ever since have found various expressions of accountability within their own respective structures. But above all, leaders must answer to God.

Leaders are not free to lead as they want. Their leadership must reflect the example of the One from whom it comes. That means leaders must walk in the way of the cross. That is what verse 7 means when it speaks of the outcome of their way of life and of their faith. If this is the case, it will not be difficult for people to come under the conviction (*peithesthai* in verse 17) that these are leaders who should be obeyed. Leadership is sacrificial. It is hard, as Paul's letters bear constant witness. It involves much work, accompanied by frequent rejection and disappointment. Anyone who signs on for leadership because they want a platform position is both dangerous and deluded.

And that brings us to the last phrase of the verse. Leaders should be able to lead with joy rather than "groaning" (verse 17d). A disrespectful or rebellious attitude among the people will be of "no advantage" to them. The health of the church community is directly linked with its submission to its leaders. How often do we spend time criticizing leaders over petty preferences and failing to realize we are damaging our relationship with the Lord himself by doing so? How easy it is to find fault with leaders while overlooking our own! There are certainly abusive leaders, and they will have to give account to God. But most elders and shepherds in the body of Christ are godly people doing a frequently thankless job. Let's set them free from that misery and give them reason to rejoice instead! We will all be the beneficiaries. Is there a cost to our freedom and independence? Yes, there is. Have they also given up an even greater measure of freedom in order to serve the flock? Yes, almost certainly. If we all surrender our freedom, will God give us greater liberty in the Holy Spirit? Yes, without doubt he will. And we will have the joy of seeing the church grow and the kingdom extended.

1 So I exhort the elders among you, as a fellow elder and a witness of the sufferings of Christ, as well as a partaker in the glory that is going to be revealed: 2 shepherd the flock of God that is among you, exercising oversight, not under compulsion, but willingly, as God would have you; not for shameful gain, but eagerly; 3 not domineering over those in your charge, but being examples to the flock. 4 And when the chief Shepherd appears, you will receive the unfading crown of glory. 5 Likewise, you who are younger, be subject to the elders. Clothe yourselves, all of you, with humility toward one another, for "God opposes the proud but gives grace to the humble." (1 Pet. 5:1-5)

Peter also addresses the issue of freedom and submission in the church. He takes care in this passage to link eldership with the sufferings of Christ. Leaders unprepared to suffer will not receive the reward. Anyone aspiring to church leadership for reasons of personal recognition or gain, or who is merely seeking the approval by others, should be disqualified. The route to eternal glory goes only one way — through the cross. On this basis, Peter addresses the elders of the churches. Leadership is a call which involves surrendering their freedom, and doing so willingly. They are to shepherd the flock of God (verse 1). The flock belongs to God, not them. As shepherds, they follow the Great Shepherd who laid down his life for the sheep. Leadership is costly, but so was the cross. Grace is free, but it is not cheap. It came at a price. And they are to shepherd not because they have to, but "willingly" or voluntarily — because they choose to (verse 2). According to Jewish theology, "volunteers" were those people who put themselves at God's disposal, either for war (Judg. 5:2) or for sacrifice (Ps. 54:6). Leadership involves both spiritual warfare and great sacrifice. God has always acted toward us voluntarily — that is the very meaning of grace. Paul appealed to Philemon to set Onesimus free voluntarily (Philem. verse 14). Elders should accept their call voluntarily. They choose to give themselves into God's service, which involves both war and sacrifice, including the sacrifice of their personal freedom. Their motivation must never be for "shameful gain." Elders should be financially supported if they are serving full time, but their heart must never be tainted by greed. They are not to domineer, but to be examples to the flock (verse 3). The word "domineer" comes from the same root as the word *kurios* or "lord." Jesus is the only Lord, and leaders are not to usurp his place. There is a reward to leadership, but we are not to look for it primarily in this life. It is not an Olympic crown of human recognition, or a gold crown of wealth, but an eternal crown of glory (verse 4).

But Peter, like Paul and the author of Hebrews, never forgets to remind us that leaders are to be honored and obeyed. Those who are younger and less mature in the faith are particularly admonished here to be subject to the elders (verse 5a). Those who are older and more mature hopefully need less reminding. One of the great tragedies in the body of Christ is the premature promotion of younger men into prominent leadership, usually on the basis of a charismatic leadership gift of one sort or the other, but without the character needed to carry the mantle. The lure of praise and power leads to disappointment or even destruction. God can take fifty years to prepare a person for the ten years he wishes to use them most strategically. Even Jesus did not begin ministry until the last three years of his life. Clearly that was not a character issue, but it still illustrates the point. Even as God's ways are not ours, neither is his timing. God's design for leadership is based on character that in normal circumstances can only come through the refining fire of discipleship and testing. This is not a prohibition of young leaders. It's just a call for rebalancing practices which have got many leaders and churches into trouble unnecessarily and sometimes tragically. Always place younger leaders under the authority of those more seasoned, and then they can be released in their gifting safely.

Peter concludes with an appeal for all of us to clothe ourselves in humility (verse 5b). The phrase is used of slaves putting on a tunic to keep themselves from becoming dirty while serving. Peter may well be thinking back to the night Jesus took up the towel to wash his disciples' feet. The place of greatest freedom is not when all of us expand our spheres of independence to the maximum degree possible. It is when we lay our independence down and serve one another, when our lives become truly subject to the truth that sets us free. That is the paradox of the kingdom. But in it is found true freedom.

FOURTEEN

LESSONS IN FREEDOM
FROM THE PANDEMIC

In 1905, a day when courts were far more influenced by Biblical thinking than they are today, the United States Supreme Court rendered a judgment on the contentious issue of smallpox vaccination. Justice John Marshall Harlan wrote the following words on behalf of the Court: "Real liberty for all could not exist under the operation of a principle which recognizes the right of each individual person to use his own, whether in respect of his person or his property, regardless of the injury that may be done to others." This decision justified mandatory smallpox vaccinations. The context, of course, was different to that of the debates over mandatory vaccination arising from the COVID pandemic. COVID is not smallpox, and today there is far more reason for concern over government overreach than there was in 1905. Nevertheless, the Biblical framework behind the Court's decision has not changed, and this gives Christians some big questions to grapple with.

These are not questions created by the pandemic, though the pandemic has certainly brought them into sharper focus. They have been growing in significance for many years, as Christian influence and values in society have progressively diminished, and Christians in the west and even in North America adjust to a world a little more like that of their brothers and sisters elsewhere. This is not necessarily a bad thing, as Christianity is at its best when it is a counter-cultural movement. But the pandemic has certainly brought to the forefront a debate over the proper exercise of freedom, and not only among believers. Christians, of all people, however, should be able to understand how to conduct themselves in such a debate, yet sadly many have not progressed any further than the kind of demanding of rights we turn around and condemn in others.

I will try to connect some of the dots in this book together in order to provide some practical guidance. The political problems we face today did not arise out of nowhere. The problem of government overreach is directly connected with the increasingly pervasive influence of a fatalistic culture in which each group vies for their rights at the expense of the others. Various groups enlist the power of the state on their behalf, and in due course, as it was with the battle over abortion fifty years ago, might becomes right, and the most defenseless lose. The Christian Gospel tells a very different story, one of a loving God who sent his Son to die for undeserving people. It calls those who follow that Son to walk in his footsteps. The Gospel is about giving up rights, not acquiring them, still less at the expense of others.

The Gospel tells us of a personal Creator God who fashioned each person in his own image. The moment we grasp this truth, we are set free from the power of an impersonal fate, whether that fate is conceived of as the ancient Greeks did, or in the form of modern materialistic physics. Fate is an impersonal system which offers a limited pie, one in which each person scrambles to secure their fair share. That's bad enough. But when you add to the mix a dose of modern Marxism in its current form of critical or social justice theory, it gets worse. That is because the latter philosophies fashion people into groups of oppressor and oppressed classes. Marx saw this simply in economic terms, but his present-day heirs have expanded that to affect almost every realm of life. If you consider everyone under average income to be oppressed, all women to be oppressed, and everyone who is not white to be oppressed, even before you get to the issue of sexual orientation or people who suffer from various disadvantages or disabilities, you have categorized well over 90% of the world's population as part of an oppressed class which should be seeking the means to enlarge their share of the pie. Postmodernism thus sets large portions of the population against each other. It has already begun to lead to social chaos and disintegration in cities and regions where it has gained the most influence. Out the other end of the power struggle will emerge another set of winners and losers, but one thing there won't be is worldwide equality!

In the midst of this cultural and social hurricane, Christians who claim the Gospel supports their political or economic views must be very careful in the claims they make. Pilate assumed Jesus had a political and economic agenda, and Jesus answered his question with great precision: "My kingdom is not of this world" (Jn. 19:36). This is not to say the Gospel is not to have any impact on the world in which we live. Most of our hospitals and many of our educational institutions were founded by Christians applying the Gospel to the practical needs they saw around them. Our western legal systems were fashioned largely on a Biblical foundation of justice. Respect for the rights of each person as equal before God comes directly from the Bible. This includes the recognition that the powers of government must be exercised in the service of its citizens, not as the means of lording it over them. The more power government accumulates, the more temptation there is to concentrate that power in the hands of the few who control it.

So there are plenty of reasons for Christians of various political persuasions to exercise a role in society, but their primary motivation should be the well-being of others, even if that comes at our own expense.

The Covid pandemic has given us a great opportunity to examine some of these questions from a Biblical viewpoint. The first and greatest problem many Christians face arises from a distorted eschatology. A friend remarked to me in seminary that our eschatology affects everything else we believe. At the time, his comment passed over my head but as the years have passed, I realize how correct he was. Dispensationalism is a relatively recent innovation, but has attained enormous influence in many parts of the world. It paints a picture of a world awaiting demonic rule, a world out of which God must rescue his people, much like governments airlifted citizens out of Vietnam in 1975 or Afghanistan in 2021. For as long as I have been a Christian, people have been looking for signs of the end and the rising of the Antichrist. In spite of one prediction after another proving false, so-called prophets, instead of repenting, simply make further predictions. I explain in detail in my book *Mystery Explained: A Simple Guide to Revelation* why this whole system is so thoroughly unbiblical. My point here is simply to underline its practical effect: *Christians have become so focused on a coming Satanic rule they have lost sight of the sovereignty of an Almighty God over his creation.* And as a result, they have fallen into fear, and have become sitting ducks for every conspiracy theory that comes along, most of which come not from within the church, but from the pagan culture around us. It is impossible to conduct a reasoned or balanced conversation about the merits or demerits of a vaccine once you have become convinced Bill Gates has placed a microchip into it as a direct fulfillment of the prophecies of Revelation. It is impossible to conduct a reasoned or balanced conversation about the actions of government once you have become convinced it is controlled through some back-room conspiracy by the Antichrist. The twisted and unbiblical eschatology of multitudes of Christians has prevented them from seeing truth from the perspective of a sovereign God rather than a sovereign devil.

During the pandemic period, many people, including Christians, raised sincere concerns about the rapid development of vaccines, and whether it is wise to take them or not. That is a separate question, yet it cannot be divorced from the Biblical command to place the interests of others ahead of our own. The real question a Christian has to face is not whether we can demand the right to refuse vaccination, but whether we can demand the right to work or study in an environment where we may give mortal offence to unbelievers who, without the assurance and comfort of the Holy Spirit in their lives, are living in fear we might transmit a deadly illness to them. Paul warned the strong believers not to exercise their freedom in such a way that they made the weak believers stumble. How much more responsibility do we have to exercise our freedom very carefully when our actions are affecting people who do not know Christ at all! Our lives and conduct are the only Bible they will read. It will not be easy to balance our worries about what we might see as a too-hastily developed vaccine with the concern to be a Christ-like witness to our neighbor, but we must make the effort, for eternal stakes are involved in the lives of those around us.

A further issue is the possible overreach of governments. In the United Kingdom during the second world war, citizens were required to carry identity cards. This was deemed to be an emergency measure due to the threat to national security posed by the circumstances. The war ended, but governments were reluctant to surrender the rights they had acquired. It took a court case to free citizens of an exercise of governmental power justified in wartime but not in peacetime. The problem we have with government overreach is the influence not of incorrect eschatology, but of misguided philosophy. The postmodern obsession with the acquiring of rights has led to pressure groups attempting to hijack governments in order to change the rules to favor them and give them a bigger piece of the pie. When various groups are attempting this, even though some of them have competing interests, *the overall effect is to enlarge the role of government and reduce the freedoms of individual citizens.* This has certainly been one impact of critical theory, as governments and even corporations have been enlisted in the social justice cause. This has given rise to legitimate concern, and not only among Christians.

According to Romans 13, Christians are called to respect the role of government. In a free society, part of this responsibility is to be involved in the democratic process to advocate for the rights of others, not just our own. In turn, this should lead Christians to oppose an overreach of governmental power where it would become harmful to the well being of the majority of citizens. Above all, it means Christians should advocate for the most defenseless of all, those not yet born. It is impossible to reconcile a profession of belief in Christ while advocating for or even tolerating the slaughter of unborn babies. It is truly a latter-days holocaust. That much is clear, or should be. How this applies to a far more nuanced question like governments mandating vaccines is more complex. It is quite possible to take the position in relation to vaccines that it is most often a good witness, and quite likely common sense, to take the vaccine, while at the same time advocating for the rights of citizens to make decisions regarding their own medical care in a way they feel comfortable with.

In all these matters, God is most interested in the attitude of our hearts. Paul wrote these words to the Philippians: "Do nothing from selfish ambition or conceit, but in humility count others more significant than yourselves. Let each of you look not only to his own interests, but also to the interests of others. Have this mind among yourselves, which is yours in Christ Jesus, who, though he was in the form of God, did not count equality with God a thing to be grasped, but emptied himself, by taking the form of a servant, being born in the likeness of men. And being found in human form, he humbled himself by becoming obedient to the point of death, even death on a cross" (Phil. 2:3-8). The question then becomes focused not on my rights or desires, but on the well-being of my neighbor, the one for whom Christ died. How do I walk that out as a friend, neighbor, co-worker or fellow student? How do I walk that out with my brothers and sisters in Christ? Paul held the firm belief that Jesus had declared all foods clean, yet was willing to forego eating meat if it caused his weaker brother to fall. The fact he was free on the inside enabled him to forego the outward exercise of his freedom if it served the well-being of his neighbor.

There is no exact template for us to walk out our faith in the midst of a society torn by pandemic strife and personal tragedy, not to mention cataclysmic social upheaval due to the fatalistic and destructive influence of postmodernism. Yet there is a reliable and trustworthy guide in the Scriptures, taught by godly leaders and applied to our hearts by the Holy Spirit. *If the mind of Christ is in us, the conduct of Christ will surely shape us.* That is another reason for churches to return to a far deeper teaching of Scripture than has often been the case.

And it is that Scripture, not ancient or modern philosophers or scientists, which tells us where true freedom is to be found:

16 But when one turns to the Lord, the veil is removed. 17 Now the Lord is the Spirit, and where the Spirit of the Lord is, there is freedom. 18 And we all, with unveiled face, beholding the glory of the Lord, are being transformed into the same image from one degree of glory to another. For this comes from the Lord who is the Spirit.

The veil Paul is referring to is what covered the face of Moses so that the people could not see the glory of the Lord as he came out of God's presence.

The Lord who revealed himself to Moses is Yahweh. But now this Lord — Yahweh — is revealed to us in the person of the Holy Spirit ("the Lord is the Spirit"). When we turn to the Spirit, "the veil is removed." We can resist the Spirit (Ac. 7:51), grieve the Spirit (Eph. 4:30) or even insult the Spirit (Heb. 10:29). But we can also turn to the Spirit by responding to his presentation of the gospel to our hearts.

And where the Spirit of the Lord is, there is freedom. The word "freedom" has no article attached to it. That means this is freedom in the widest possible sense. It is *freedom from* the veil (verses 14-16), from hardness of heart (verses 13-14), and from the condemnation of the law (verse 6). But it is also *freedom for* beholding God's glory, identifying with Christ, and being transformed into his likeness (verse 18). This privilege is accorded not just to one person, as in the old covenant, but to all of us ("we all"). Our faces have been "unveiled." The word expresses a permanent and irreversible action. The one God saves he also keeps. We are now "beholding" God's glory and "being transformed." These phrases refer to an ongoing daily experience. Our receiving of the Spirit in our conversion has set us on a daily, lifelong exodus out of slavery and into the glory of God. Every day this journey takes us further into freedom. And the One who gives this incredible freedom is the Holy Spirit: "all this comes from the Lord who is the Spirit."

Charismatics have often unwittingly trivialized this verse to suggest that the experience of spiritual gifts is what brings true freedom. But that is not what Paul is saying at all. *He is talking about a whole new life God has given us. It is* life in the Spirit. Whether or not we exercise charismatic gifts, we all participate in the new life the Spirit has given us. The content of this life is what we have tried to describe in this book. It is a journey of freedom, freedom from the condemnation of the law, freedom from the power of sin and ultimately freedom from death. Every day it leaves

Egypt further and further behind. It is also a journey which brings us into freedom for obedience to God's law and to Christ. Every day it takes us closer and closer to the Promised Land.

The pagan culture in which we live is increasingly based on a zero-sum mentality: I gain at your expense. This is not freedom, but slavery. Christian freedom takes us down a path pagan culture cannot even begin to comprehend: you gain at my expense. That is what the cross is all about. It initiates a new exodus, this time one with eternal consequences. God the Father placed the cross at the center of his plan to restore humanity. You can fight it or ignore it, but you will lose. The way to true freedom is found only at the foot of the cross. Playing zero-sum games simply means that in the end both parties lose. The losing party suffers loss, while the winning party becomes a lonely person because no one wants to be close enough to them to get hurt themselves. It is an all too frequent tragedy where marriages, families, friendships and even whole societies wind up in this condition.

God has provided a better way, described in these chapters. It is the road out of slavery and into freedom. Wise people will take it.

ABOUT THE AUTHOR

From the Toronto region. David holds three degrees in theology. He and his wife, Elaine, have planted churches in the UK and Canada. David also teaches internationally in churches, Bible colleges, leadership training centers, and the online platforms TheosUniversity and TheosSeminary. David and Elaine have eight children and eight grandchildren which, let's be honest, is an accomplishment.

NIGHT LIGHT
How to Find God in the Midst of Suffering

By David Campbell

JOY COMES IN THE MORNING. FIND HOPE IN THE NIGHT.

Why are we scared of the dark? Usually it's because we don't know what's there. Perhaps a friend? Perhaps a foe? The Bible tells us that even though we "walk through the valley of the shadow of death," God is with us. In this topical look at Christian suffering, author David Campbell reminds us that God has purpose in every season – even the painful ones. Both provocative and comprehensive, Night Light will give you a foundation of strength to walk through the most challenging circumstances.

OTHER TITLES BY DAVID CAMPBELL

No Diving
10 Ways to Avoid the Shallow End of your Faith and Go Deeper Into the Bible

By David Campbell

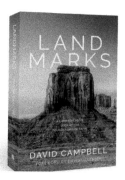

Landmarks
A Comprehensive Look at the Foundations of Faith

By David Campbell

Mystery Explained
A Simple Guide to Revelation

By David Campbell

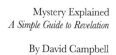

All titles available from Amazon or from unprecedentedpress.com/shop

Lightning Source UK Ltd.
Milton Keynes UK
UKHW021812220922
409257UK00006B/84